ANXIOUSLY EVER AFTER

AN HONEST MEMOIR ON MENTAL ILLNESS,
STRAINED RELATIONSHIPS, AND EMBRACING THE STRUGGLE

ANXIOUSLY EVER AFTER

CLINT EDWARDS

AUTHOR OF FATHER-ISH, SILENCE IS A SCARY SOUND,
AND I'M SORRY...LOVE, YOUR HUSBAND

PAGE STREET
PUBLISHING CO.

PAGE STREET
PUBLISHING CO.

FOR MEL.

AUTHOR'S NOTE

Names and identifying characteristics have been
changed to protect identities. Dialogue and order
of events have been reconstructed according to my
memory, along with conversations with those who
were there. I have taken great care to present the
truth as I remember it.

Nobody heard him, the dead man,
But still he lay moaning:
I was much further out than you thought
And not waving but drowning.

—STEVIE SMITH

CONTENTS

Foreword   12

Everything Changed   20

PART 1: MY INHERITANCE   29

The Clubhouse   30

Where Dad Lived   67

"I Don't Believe You"   77

Bad Ass Coffee   110

Elephant   122

PART 2: OBSESSIVE-COMPULSIVE DISORDER   137

I Have No Plans. Not a Single One.   138

Drugs at a Toy Store   150

"Let's Hope You Don't Become Him"   169

Footsteps   175

PART 3: LIVING WITH DENIAL 197

Tick, Tick, Tock 198

"You Can Go . . ." 214

A Feeling I Hadn't Expected 231

When Feelings of Failure Are in Vogue 245

"What Are You Afraid Of?" 261

PART 4: FINDING BALANCE 272

I May Never Be Happy 273

Embarrassment Looks a Lot Like an
Emotional Breakdown 278

Let's Address That Childhood Trauma,
Shall We? 296

Unpacking My Father 309

EPILOGUE 320

Their Inheritance 321

EPILOGUE: PART 2 326

You're Doing It 327

Acknowledgments 331

About the Author 333

FOREWORD

I was first introduced to Clint's writing in his 2014 *New York Times* essay: "Getting Up in the Night Is Your Wife's Job." Briefly, in this essay, Clint and his wife Mel are new parents, both working, exhausted and juggling the new adjustments of being parents of an infant. In a conversation between Clint and his mother, when Clint shared that he was waking up in the middle of the night to care for their infant son, his mother imposed judgment on Mel. She said that getting up in the night was his wife's job. And initially, Clint took in his mom's belief for a moment. Then he paused, reflected, and shared with incredible vulnerability: He gets up in the middle of the night to care for his child in reaction to the pain and abandonment he felt in childhood from his father. For Clint, getting up in the middle of the night to care for his child was an act of love, and healing, embracing what it meant for him to be a father and supportive husband. I observed, caring for his son was a drive to heal from his father's actions and inactions.

I remember vividly feeling chills reading Clint's essay, reflecting, this is what we need in the world: men, fathers, husbands, sharing their stories, showing vulnerability, and talking about mental health and suffering. And most importantly, healing from pain and suffering. Clint's essay was impactful to me as a person and psychologist, as it was a moment where I began to have hope and inspiration for males to speak about mental health and mental illness and in doing so, inspiring others to do the same. We need more male voices sharing their stories, and this book *Anxiously Ever After*, gives the reader a lens into Clint's childhood, adolescence and the impact life events had on him in his past and now, as a father and husband. Us readers, are finally able to see more in depth what Clint shared in this moving essay years ago.

Previous to reading this essay, in the world of parenting narratives, essays, blogs, and books, a vast majority of the voices I had read were from a mother's point of view. Clint was the first parenting voice I read from a husband and father and I was moved.

In my work with supporting males in the therapy hour: adolescent, young adults, husbands, fathers, and grandfathers, I hear from them in safety of the therapy hour, how challenging it can be for males to express emotions, seek help for mental health and mental illness, with a theme of shame or feeling 'less masculine' in the vulnerability of emotional and psychological challenges, struggles and symptoms that are often hidden, ignored and discouraged in our culture and society.

Clint's essays, books, and social media posts have became a beacon of light giving individuals permission to be authentic, vulnerable, and share their stories. I have been positively impacted and inspired by Clint's work so much so, that in the therapy hour, when clients share parallels to his story, impactful life events, or have apprehension to talk about mental health because of stigma about males in therapy, I weave in what Clint has shared of himself in his writing.

In the United States it is estimated 52.9 million adults experience mental illness[1]. As a psychologist, this number is almost incomprehensible, I can not wrap my brain around the vastness of this number. What helps me to understand this statistic, is to break it into something relatable to everyday life. I encourage you to do the same. One in five adults experience some level of mental illness, from mild to moderate and severe. Next time you are waiting in line at the grocery store, or seated in your child's classroom at parent-teacher night, or watching your child's soccer game on a blustery weekend morning, or when you are sitting in your house of worship attending services, or at a gathering with friends and family, or at work in a meeting or commuting to work, look around for every five adults you see, one of them has mental illness.

Mental illness doesn't always 'look' or present in individuals the way we think it does or expect. Many of us have received negative messages and beliefs about mental illness from our family, friends, society, culture, and religion, perpetuating the stigma of mental illness. In my work I frequently hear that the bias and stigma of mental illness is due to problems with one's character, or being lazy, or not trying hard enough, or feeling sorry for oneself, or focusing on the past, blaming parents and childhood, and individuals need to stop complaining and feeling sorry for themselves.

Adding to the complexity regarding the prevalence of mental illness, males experience mental illness (children, adolescents and adults); however, due to stigma and under-reporting through seeking treatment, the incidence of mental illness for males, what we know, is not an accurate number.

Males have even more challenges and complexity regarding mental illness and seeking treatment. Our society and culture perpetuates standards of 'masculinity'; what it means to be male, through norms of encouraging male power, dominance, and privilege, while discouraging and disapproving the expression of emotions for males. These stigmas and beliefs perpetuate, delay, and prevent males from talking about, seeking and engaging in treatment for mental illness[5]. When we continue to hold the belief and expectation that males shouldn't express emotions, that in doing so, males are weak, or males shouldn't seek help for mental health creates dangerous conditions for our males such as worsening symptoms of depression and anxiety, increase of substance use and dependence, increased problems in relationships such as domestic violence, diminished emotional intimacy, as well as increased rates of violence and self-harm[2]. Instead of suffering in silence, or feeling shame due to mental health issues and mental illness, we have to begin addressing the stigma associated with mental illness with special attention given to our sons, fathers, and husbands.

When I experience and hear these biases and stigmas, I often close my eyes, center myself, pause and take a deep breath before I respond with compassion and facts: mental illness is not a character flaw or deficit in a person or intentional or blaming parents and childhood experiences. Mental illness and mental health is complex, with biological factors such as what we inherit genetically and our brain chemistry, all of which is impacted by family history, life experiences and lifestyle behaviors such as nutrition, diet, exercise and other factors [3].

As a Clinical Assistant Professor in the Department of Psychiatry and Human Behavior at the Warren Alpert Medical School of Brown University, and attending psychologist at Emma Pendleton Bradley Hospital, the nation's first psychiatric hospital for children and adolescents, I provide care to adolescents on the inpatient unit. Every day I work to re-educate and break down the pervasive stigma and discrimination about mental illness with adolescent patients and their families. Individuals with mental illness are not crazy, or insane, or a failure, or damaged and broken, and neither are their parents and caregivers. These are often some of the thoughts they believe and often what they fear.

I provide a different perspective through a compassionate lens: mental illness and the symptoms individuals experience are unhealed, untreated parts of their suffering that needs some attention and intervention and support. Much like a broken bone needs a cast to heal, or someone with diabetes or high cholesterol needs to make modifications to lifestyle, such as to add medication and change nutrition and activity, mental illness needs to be brought out of the shadows of shame and personal character flaw and deficits, and spoken about, and de-stigmatized and treatment options such as psychiatric medication and therapy offered with compassionate understanding through the lens of empirically based research and science.

Unfortunately, while there have been important advances in de-stigmatizing mental illness, we as a culture and society continue to have significant work to do to continue breaking down the barriers, specifically for male children, adolescents, young adults, and adults.

Clint's memoir and sharing of his life events and journey to address and manage his mental illness is an important contribution to breaking down the stigma of males talking about mental illness and seeking treatment options to heal and manage mental health.

When I read work from a person that moves and inspires me, as Clint has done for years, where he provides a lens into what it means to navigate the challenges in life and what it means to be human, I bring those stories, memoirs, and essays into the therapy room with the goal: sharing with clients and patients that they are not alone, here is a story that will help them on their journey.

We heal through connection, reducing isolation, judgement and having supportive people to go along with us on our journey of healing. Clint's book, *Anxiously Ever After*, may be the most impactful work he has created to date, helping to reduce the stigma of mental illness for young boys, adolescents, and men, through sharing with readers the vulnerability, challenges and adverse life events he experienced in childhood and adolescence, and how these experiences continue to impact him as an adult, husband, and father. He is impacted yet not defined by these experiences, which is a reminder that many of us have suffered and continue to need to heal as we move along this journey in life.

Perpetuating beliefs and stigma about mental illness is harmful leading to negative impact on individuals diagnosed with mental illness showing up in the form of reduced hope, low self-esteem and self-worth, increased intensity of mental illness symptoms, difficulties in relationships and functioning in school or work, and delaying treatment and seeking support for distressing symptoms of mental illness[2].

And one way you can begin to break down the stigma and negative beliefs you may hold about mental illness is to open your heart and continue reading this book. And share this book with anyone you know struggling with mental illness or adverse childhood experiences that are continuing to impact them as adults and parents. Share it with the male children, adolescents, husbands and fathers. And give them the reassurance: you are not alone, you do not have to suffer in silence, and while we are impacted by our experiences, we don't have to be defined by them.

Clint's book is notable—you will read it and perhaps relate to some of his childhood and adolescence experiences, or perhaps his struggles as a father and husband, or perhaps you will read his story and say to yourself, I had no idea this is what he went through, he seems to have it all. To which I ask you to look within your heart and mind and embrace a new way of understanding mental illness. Individuals are more than their mental illness, more than a diagnosis, more than the events or circumstance of life events and experiences. And most importantly, as Clint has so beautifully shared, living with mental illness is a journey, and while we are impacted by our life events, we do not have to be defined by our experiences, as we can heal and grow and create one beautiful and meaningful life for ourselves and our children.

–Claire Nicogossian, Psy. D.,
Clinical Assistant Professor at Brown University
and author of *Mama, You Are Enough*

1.   https://www.nimh.nih.gov/health/statistics/mental-illness#part_154910

2.   https://www.psychiatry.org/patients-families/stigma-and-discrimination

3.   https://medlineplus.gov/mentalhealth.html

4.   https://www.apa.org/about/policy/boys-men-practice-guidelines.pdf

5.   https://www.ncbi.nlm.nih.gov/pmc/articles/PMC7444121/

EVERYTHING CHANGED

I grew up in west Provo, Utah, within a stone's throw of the city-county border. Provo is part of Utah County, which is, apparently, the solid brass buckle of the Book of Mormon belt. I'd like you to know that is a real thing. I didn't make it up for this book, although I do wish I was clever enough to coin a catchy term like *Book of Mormon belt*. You can Google it—there's a Wikipedia page and everything, making it 100 percent factual.

And if you do Google it, you will also discover that the Book of Mormon belt is sometimes called the Jell-O belt, because Mormons have a thing for Jell-O, which I can confirm is true. There has been tons of it at every church potluck I've ever attended. This all means that if I extend the belt-buckle metaphor to the Jell-O belt, then I actually grew up in of one of those vintage circular Jell-O molds that were so popular at church parties in the '80s. But, unlike the Mormons at those parties, I've never really liked Jell-O. It's the texture. It's slimy and I can't eat it without gagging, and sometimes I wonder if this reaction to Jell-O makes me a jack Mormon. Naturally, this is another uniquely Mormon term that I have chosen not to cover in this book (you can Google it on your own, I suppose, but it is—believe it or not—an entry in *Merriam-Webster*).

Anyway, I'm digressing, and according to my editor, that's not a good thing to do on the first page of a book. What I want to get across, though, is that I'd never heard of the Book of Mormon belt as a kid because I was living in it. Mormonism, Mormon culture, and Jell-O were my normal until I went to graduate school in Minnesota, and only then did I fully realize how freaking weird I was. (Although, to be fair, being Mormon was only about 20 percent of my weirdness. The majority of my oddness will be discussed later on.)

And I suppose the reason I am bringing all of this up is to help you understand that I lived an incredibly "white bread, church on Sunday, no R-rated movies, no one drinking coffee or booze or using tobacco, mom manages the home and dad works long hours, families that pray together stay together" sort of life until I was nine. That's when my father came home and told the family he'd been having an affair, and he wanted a divorce.

I eventually found out his new flame was Catholic. Not that there's anything wrong with being Catholic. There isn't. It's just that I'd never met someone who was Catholic, or Jewish, or Protestant, or Muslim, or Buddhist, or any other faith outside of Mormonism. And at the age of nine, I honestly wondered if other religions were

CLINT EDWARDS

just some fictional story played out on TV, because in my world everyone was Mormon. We all had a married mother and father, and adultery was one of the never-happens, no-one-would-ever sins.

When I discovered my dad was having an affair, I'm not sure how much I even understood the word. I had two connections with it: My religion said it was über wrong, and my sister watched *Beverly Hills, 90210* pretty religiously, and I'm 90 percent sure one of the parents on that show had an affair, and I remember thinking, *Well, that person is going to hell, and fast, and on a rocket ship.*

And in so many ways, when I look back on that day, it felt like the real world—the one outside of Mormonism and the Book of Mormon belt—came strolling into my house, looking and acting like my father. But clearly this was Mr. Hyde.

Apparently they met at some mom-and-pop diner located below a viaduct on the east side of town. They'd fallen in love, and now he just didn't have time for my mother anymore, or me.

Well, I suppose he didn't say those exact words, but that's how it felt. I don't remember exactly what he said the day he told us about the affair and left. I remember feeling very scared and unsure, almost like my life was approaching a cliff and, without my having voice in the matter, some unseen force was going to toss me over the precipice and into a dark, unknown place where my parents were divorced, something I didn't have a script for.

To my knowledge, I was about to become the only kid outside of my older half-sister and older half-brother, a boy I'd met only a handful of times, that had divorced parents. Mom and Dad were each on their second marriage. I knew that, but I honestly don't remember when I learned that information.

I can remember my parents arguing over paying child support to my father's first wife, but I can't recall the details. And I can't remember my sister ever visiting her father, or even speaking about him. It felt like he never existed. Doing the math, she was sixteen, and my parents had been married for fifteen years, meaning she must have been one or two when my mother and her father separated. The family we shared was the only family she'd ever known. I hadn't seen my older half-brother in years, and sadly, my father didn't talk about him. Like my sister's father, it felt like he didn't exist.

We didn't talk about the past, so those previous marriages felt like something that I knew happened but were a million miles away from me, my family, and my day-to-day life. I had one full biological brother, Trent, with whom I was close. He was twelve. I was the youngest, and from my point of view at the age of nine, my family was this little solid unit that fit well with the others in our Mormon community.

But suddenly I was about to become the only boy at church, at school, and on my baseball and wrestling teams with divorced parents. I felt like I had no one I could approach and commiserate with: "Yo, man. Your parents are divorced. Want to hang out and talk about how amazing and heartbreaking it is to have two Christmases?"

Nope.

No one.

I'll tell you what I do remember from that night. My mother sitting in our family Blazer in the garage, mascara streaming down her face, her permed bleached-blond hair a mess because she'd been rubbing her palms through it, her hands at ten and two on the steering wheel—almost like she was going to drive somewhere, but ultimately did not have anywhere to go.

And I remember Dad in the bedroom as he packed a duffel bag full of polyester button-up western-style shirts, polo shirts with his sheet-metal company's logo above the right chest pocket, Wrangler jeans, Stetson cologne, and what must have been dozens and dozens of bottles of prescription painkillers that he'd collected over the past few years.

And what I remember most vividly is that, as he packed his bag, I wrote him a poem on a blue sticky note I found on the kitchen counter. I had my older sister check the spelling. I handed him the poem just before he walked out the door. He was sitting at the table cramming his feet into a pair of scuffed leather work boots. Then he slid his tight western-style pant legs over the boot shaft, his silver square-framed glasses sliding to the end of his nose, his jaw square and tight with conviction and his short black hair falling into his face, the duffel bag sitting next to him.

He let out a huff. But it wasn't a "I need to be here for you, son" sort of expression or an "I'm sorry about all this" sort of moment but more of an "I just need this chapter to be closed" sort of feeling.

The note was folded, so he opened it with that slender and calloused left hand that I'd gotten so used to holding as a child. He tilted his head back, his face clean-shaven, and pulled his hair to the side so he could read my poem with his bifocals.

ROSES ARE RED,

VIOLETS ARE BLUE.

IF YOU LEAVE MOM,

I WILL BE BLUE TOO.

He looked at me over the top of the note, and for one moment I felt confident that I'd turned the tide, changed his heart, and that he'd unpack his bag.

But he didn't.

He scoffed, tossed it on the table, finished putting on his boots, and walked out the door without saying a word to me.

And I remember just standing there, listening to Mom crying in the garage, my sister and brother now crying in their rooms. I heard Dad turn over the motor on his pickup, pop it into gear, and back out of the driveway.

And then it was quiet for a while. It was a swampy, heavy silence, and I remember wondering, *Who the heck was that guy?*

Because I didn't recognize him anymore.

And what I need you to understand is that until

this moment, I could say, unequivocally, without any sort of hesitation, that I loved my dad.

He was a great hugger. I cannot understate that. He was one of those dads that crouched down with a big warm smile, and said "Come 'ere, boy!" I'd run into his arms, and he'd wrap them around me, squeeze me so hard I lost a breath, pick me up for the crescendo, squeezing a little harder, seal it with a kiss on my forehead, and then set me down, his arms open, almost like he'd just put the last strip of frosting on a prize-winning cake.

He was one of those cool dads—he'd let me use power tools, or he'd slap a welding mask on my small face and let me place a few beads with the arc welder, or he'd buy me the king-sized candy bar and a jumbo fountain drink at the gas station just because, or he'd allow me to ride in the bed of the pickup truck on farm roads, all of it under the condition of "don't tell your mother." He had this warm, affectionate laugh that I adored as a child. He was a chronic tickler. The kind of guy that might, without warning, pinch my knee in the middle of a quiet movie theater, just to see me squirm and cry out in laughter.

Sometimes we played this game he called "tickle hands." He'd put his hands in his pockets and then pull them out dramatically, like we were in a Billy the Kid–style gunfight, and then he'd sprint at me with his fingers flailing. I'd run away, squealing, but never fast enough to get away. I absolutely loved it when he caught me. Even all these years later, I can't help but smile as I write about this.

About a year before he left, he took my older full brother, Trent, and I into the backyard and helped us build this pretty sweet clubhouse. Just the three of us. I mean, sure, it wasn't much more than a one-bedroom box made from cedar fence posts and two-by-fours, but for my brother and I, it was this huge amazing space that was just for us, away from our parents, where we could let our imaginations run wild and make off-color fart jokes and talk freely about our misunderstandings of the adult world. He showed me how to use a hammer, a power saw, and a tape measure, and I remember finishing that clubhouse with him and feeling comfortable and safe and grounded, knowing that he was my dad and he'd always be there to teach me.

And while he didn't always make it to my baseball games, when he did, he was without a doubt the loudest person in the stands—obnoxiously so—cheering me on and asking the coach to put me in because I was *the* star player. Which, to be honest, was in direct contrast with reality, because I sucked pretty hard at baseball, never actually hitting a pitch or catching a ball. And sometimes I cried when they made me run laps, which, according to *A League of Their Own*, is against the rules of baseball. My throw was pathetic (it still is), and when I did get put into a game, I would almost always be placed in deep right field next to the freeway, because the coach, my teammates, God, everyone knew that I was a short, pudgy, pigeon-toed kid with the hand-eye coordination of a drunk honey badger. And yet my father saw none of this, and I couldn't help but feel like a future All-American through his eyes.

And I know it's hard to look at life and say, "This was the moment. This was when it all changed." Because real life doesn't exactly have distinct turning points. It's more of a gradual thing, where people make decisions that lead to other decisions, and it all plays out slowly. But the day my father admitted he was having an affair and walked out, my life changed forever.

PART 1

MY INHERITANCE

THE CLUBHOUSE

Dad was a licensed heating and air-conditioning contractor, and behind our house was his tan and brown shop. We lived on a one-acre lot that was originally part of my paternal grandfather's beef farm, so we were surrounded by barbed wire fences, grass, and black and white Holstein cattle lazily chewing their cud. We lived in central Utah, so the summers were hot, dry, and bright, and the grass, and the weeds, and the mountains in the distance were the same yellow as the siding on our yellow and red brick home by mid-June, and they stayed that color until the snow fell around Halloween, turning everything white.

Our house was one floor, three bedrooms, and maybe 2,000 square feet. The shop was surrounded by gravel, while the house had a healthy lawn. I have to admit, Dad was a hardworking dude. He got to work early, long before the sun, banging on sheet metal and firing up welders and exhaust fans. He always worked with both of the shop's large brown garage doors open, fans blowing, while jamming out to the local country station KKAT. He worked late, and not much got in the way of his labor. If he smacked his thumb with a hammer, he threw the hammer and got back to work. If his jeans caught fire because of a spark from the welding torch, he did a little dance to put it out and went back to welding. He stayed in the shop, working away, until long after the sun went down.

And in the days after Dad left my mother, he just kept going to work in the backyard, same as he always did, almost like the whole experience wasn't more significant than smacking his thumb. My brother, sister, and I went to school. A year or so before Dad left, Mom got a part-time job collecting payments at the power company as a way to make extra money. But after Dad left, she started working there full-time.

If I were a neighbor looking from across the street (not that we had more than two neighbors that could easily see our home), it would look like nothing had changed. But nothing was the same after the night Dad walked out. Sometimes he'd show up to work, all smiles, his hair combed, and he'd strut around the shop the same as he always had before. Sometimes he'd be the same old Dad I knew and loved—he'd signal me to cross the yard, and he'd break from work to give me one of his signature hugs. And during those times, I'd tell him I missed him and wanted him to come home.

He'd always respond in that rural Utah twang of his, "Ya know I can't do that, bud. I just can't." I thought a lot about asking him why, but I was afraid to, and most of it had to do with the times when he didn't hug me.

There were days, a lot of them actually, when he'd show up, his face unshaven, clothing wrinkled, shirt untucked, hair a greasy mess, looking like he crawled out of a garbage disposal. On those days, even at the age of nine, I knew there was something terribly wrong with my father. I didn't know what, but I was afraid to ask, almost like the truth—whatever it might be—was worse than not knowing.

And if I'm being completely honest, I'd known something was wrong for a while.

Several years earlier, Dad had had an accident with a table saw. He severed four fingers from his right hand. They were crudely reattached, minus the middle knuckle, making his right hand stiff and crooked, and when he drove his pickup truck he had to hook the shifter with his thumb rather than his fingers.

Then there were the surgeries. A couple of hernia operations and a few to try to make his hand more usable. But the one I remember most clearly was on his stomach. It was to remove an ulcer. I don't remember the day he went into the hospital or the day he came out. And I don't remember the weeks he lounged in bed moaning and watching daytime TV. But what I do remember is the scar that traced from his sternum to his belly button. It was pink, crude, and bubbled like beads in an arc weld. And I remember the later surgeries, the ones my older brother tells me were a result of complications. But I've never really understood what those complications were.

That year I celebrated my eighth birthday next to Dad's hospital bed. I opened my gifts in a small hospital room, sitting on a chair next to an IV bag, as Dad slept, his bed elevated, his hands laced atop the cuff of a blue hospital blanket. He slept with his mouth open, inhaling with a smacking sound, his eyes closed, his face strained like someone treading hard to keep their head above water. I remember him returning from the hospital a couple weeks later, his weary legs struggling up the front steps.

And I remember very clearly Dad sitting on the living room floor one afternoon, shoeless, his back against the base of the sofa, his legs crisscross applesauce. I sat next to him. We were alone. The room was reflected in our weighty wooden RCA home theater. Dad stared past his reflection, eyes like a one-way mirror, and I felt certain something was hidden behind his gaze: images or shadows or something that explained his confused look. With his face closer to mine than necessary, he whispered a secret. "I feel really good," he said. "Pretty dang okay." He slouched, mouth twisted, head to the side, lips smacking with each suck of air. His eyes drifted shut, but his lazy smirk kept resurfacing, sloppy and leaning to one side.

His words slurred from time to time after that. He lost his balance in department stores and had to lean against the shelves. Sometimes he drove off the road and into the gravel, catching himself just before plowing into a barbed wire fence, and my mother would argue with him. She'd ask if she needed to drive, and he'd wave his hand and say, "You worry too much." I can remember several times seeing him with his palms down on the kitchen counter, head dipped, legs unsteady, like he'd just spun around a dozen times in a rolling chair and then stood up. And in those moments, I'd ask him what was wrong, and he'd put up his left hand and wave it a little, telling me to be quiet. Then, after a minute or two, he'd regain himself and raise his head, give me a lazy smile, wink, and wander into another room.

By the time Dad left Mom, I could tell, even as a young boy, when he was on painkillers by looking at him: the way he walked, if he dragged his feet a little, if his eyes were glossy, if he looked mismanaged. If he was high, it was almost like we were strangers. If he was sober, I was his child again.

But things really changed the morning Dad drove me to the regional youth wrestling championship at Provo High School. It was about six months before the night he left. He swerved across lanes, his hands trembling, head sagging forward, eyes closing at stoplights. This was the worst I'd ever seen him. Arriving at the high school, Dad rested the front wheels of his Ford pickup on a parking divider.

I opened the truck door, but before I could step out, he gripped my sleeve and pulled me back into the cab. He gave me a long sloppy look, inhaled sharply, and said with a heavy slur, "You're gonna do real . . ." He paused for a moment, the words escaping him, eyes drifting shut. Then they opened again, wide and dilated. His hand still gripped my shirt. "Really. Pretty okay. Just really okay. You know that? You know, I love you. Always have. You got that?"

I didn't know what to say. I wasn't sure if he was asking a question or stating a fact, so I said, "Okay."

Dad held onto my shirt and said, "No. You're not getting it. You just don't . . . get it. You're my boy. You're my boy. Always will be." He kept repeating it, "Boy, you're mine. You're my boy. Will be always." But the words kept changing order and he was speaking like he was in a trance. His eyes began to drift shut again.

"Yeah," I said. "I get it."

But I didn't. His confused words were a convoluted mix of recognizable phrases. I wanted nothing more than for him to just stop speaking, because everything he said seemed strange and confusing, and with each phrase I felt a pit in my stomach that I didn't understand.

We entered the gymnasium and Dad sat at the top of the bleachers next to the handrail, a fifteen-foot fall to his right. I watched him from the sideline as his head kept sagging forward, his hands showing no effort to reach forward and slow his descent. As I went into the first match, my eyes never left Dad.

I'd been wrestling for a year. I practiced at the high school each week. Whether they wanted to or not, I wrestled friends on our trampoline, the playground, and the chapel lawn. But when the whistle sounded, I went limp and allowed my competitor to pin me. I arched my neck and back to keep Dad in view. I was so afraid he was going to fall. He sagged further with each dip of his head. The referee's count seemed to take forever.

I left the competition and sat next to Dad in my dark green singlet, not taking time to change in the locker room. Each time his head dipped forward and then rolled back, his eyes drooping, I'd shake him, and he'd draw in a deep slurping breath.

"Hey," he said with a grin. "What am I doing way up here?"

And as I sat next to my father, it felt like our relationship was shifting, and I became more worried about managing him than managing myself. In the months between the wrestling match and Dad leaving Mom, I started keeping my eye on him when he drove me somewhere, ready to shake him if his head dipped so we could stay on the road. I watched him as he walked, feeling like I needed to catch him if he stumbled, knowing full well that I couldn't possibly hold his weight but feeling compelled to try.

And after he left my mother, I didn't see him as much, so I worried about him a lot. I worried about him driving off the road with no one to shake him awake or falling down without someone to catch him. What if he broke something and needed another surgery? That worry settled deep in my gut. It kept me up at night, feeling like I needed to watch him, but I couldn't.

After Dad left, Mom became a different person. She was a short brunette woman with bleached hair, broad shoulders, and a round nose she inherited from her mother, an immigrant from the UK. She was the kind of person who fretted a lot over the state of our house, making sure everything was clean and organized and had a place. She kind of fit the Mormon-momma stereotype in that way.

And you know, before Dad left, she was a pretty good mom. Or at least I thought so. She was the kind of mom who made your favorite meal for your birthday, no matter what it was. She was the mom who asked a lot of questions about your day at school and then sat and listened, curious about how you were doing with your friends and teachers.

I was a kid, so for the most part, she managed my schedule, buzzing me around Provo to sport practices, Cub Scouts, playdates, church activities, the works. Like my dad, she was also a pretty good hugger. She didn't crouch down and pick me up, all dramatic, like Dad did. She was more of the maternal type. She was the mom that sat down on the sofa, and you could snuggle in next to her, and she'd wrap her arm around you and then peacefully play with your hair in that simple mom way that makes every child feel completely okay with the world. There was nothing to worry about, because regardless of what was happening, there was safety in Mom's arms. I can remember her hassling me about homework, and friends, and TV shows, and sports, and all the other things I assumed everyone's mother fretted over.

She cared a great deal about appearance. I can remember many times when she'd stop me before leaving for the store. She'd take a step back, look me up and down, and say something like, "That shirt has wrinkles and a hole. Go change it." And like most kids would, I let out a huge moan and went boneless, like she'd just asked me to move a mountain, or dig a hole through the earth to Australia, or flap my arms and fly, or some other unimaginably difficult task. And she'd take my arm, drag me to my room, and find something that looked better. I'd stand there, the whole time with my shoulders slouched, like this exchange was causing me physical pain. And in these moments, she'd always say the same thing: "I just want you to look decent. I love you too much to let you walk around looking like you crawled out of a ditch."

For the most part, Mom was a consistent presence in the stands at my baseball games and my wrestling matches. She attended every single Scout Court of Honor—every single one. She'd strut up to the front of the event when I earned a rank advancement, because she knew they'd ask me to put a pin on her shirt and give her a kiss in front of everyone. I secretly loved these moments as much as she did, but I knew I couldn't let on because, you know, I had a reputation to maintain with the other boys and kissing your mother was totally uncool. Before Dad left, I felt incredibly comfortable with her. She was my mom. I defended her name on the playground and on the street corners from any sort of "your mom" joke harassment. When I was sad, hurt, bleeding, wronged, scared, down, confused, hungry, whatever—I knew I could go to her, and she'd solve all my problems, top to bottom.

But in the months after Dad left, she grew angry. Bitter. Frustrated. Hurt. Tired. And I could feel all of these emotions coming off of her, almost like steam from a pot of boiling water. Unlike Dad, she was consistent in those emotions, never wavering. I suppose she'd always had a temper, but in the past it seemed like it had had a clear reason. Her anger had a direction.

That all changed as times got harder. Dad wasn't paying child support. Mom told me about that. She mentioned it a lot, actually.

But what she never told me until almost 25 years later was that before Dad started his own business, he had a good full-time job maintaining the heating and air-conditioning system at the local hospital. But he kept running into trouble for showing up to work high on painkillers. Somehow the hospital made it a condition of his employment that he enter a drug rehabilitation program. He finished the rehabilitation program, but shortly afterward he developed an ulcer and had to have another surgery, which caused him to be prescribed more painkillers, which led to him relapsing. So the hospital fired him, and that's why he started his own business. I must have been six or seven when this was going on.

That shop behind the house? Well, after getting fired, Dad took out a bunch of loans to start his own business, and he put liens against our house and property to get those loans. And somehow my mom got wrapped up in all his business debt. He also maxed out credit cards in Mom's name before he left. It was a mess. So while my mom was working to support three kids because Dad wasn't paying child support, she was also trying to manage a mass of debt that she'd had very little say in.

That full-time job Mom had at the power company wasn't enough, so she started cleaning houses in the evenings. She would go to work before I left for school, and she often came home long after the bus had dropped me off in the afternoon. Sometimes she was warm and compassionate. Sometimes she asked about my day. Sometimes she greeted me with a hug, like she used to before Dad left. There were happy moments between us, but they weren't often, and as Mom worked longer and harder hours, those warm moments grew more and more infrequent.

I think she was just angry at the world, and her life, and the situation my father had left her in. She yelled. She yelled a lot. "What are you doing?" and "Why didn't this . . . ?" and "Why didn't that . . . ?" and "You should have done . . ."

She very clearly needed me to care for myself. I was expected to keep up with my homework, do chores around the house, make myself a healthy dinner, and pack a lunch for the following day. These were tasks I could accomplish on my own, surely. I was nine. But I was often home alone. My sixteen-year-old sister worked most evenings at a call center, and my brother was thirteen and often out with friends. So I sat at home alone, feeling anxious and lost, longing for some form of security or direction. I pined for the life I had just a couple of years earlier, when Dad was still around. I spent a lot of time trying to make sense of my father's unusual absence and behavior and feeling like I didn't have anyone to talk to. So rather than do what I was expected to do, I did absolutely nothing.

I watched TV and let my homework and chores pile up, knowing full well that I needed to pull my own weight for the sake of the situation but choosing to shut down instead.

And when I didn't do what was expected of me, the explanations, the teaching, the learning moments of youth that I was used to before Dad left didn't happen anymore. All Mom had time for were expectations, and when they weren't met, I was given scorn.

And sometimes, when she got too low, too frustrated, too depressed, she pulled a knife from the cupboards and talked about how she wanted to slit her wrists. I'd plead with her to put it down. I'd tell her I loved her and that it would be okay. But I didn't really know if it would be okay, and I don't think she did either.

Eventually she'd slam the knife into the sink, her breathing heavy, her mascara streaking down her face, her hands shaking, sweat pooling under her arms, and then she would sit on the kitchen floor with her back against the dark faux-wood cupboards, and bawl. I'd curl up next to her, and we'd sit like that, her crying and me doing what I could to comfort her. I'd tell her things would be okay, and she'd just cry and nod and say, "I know. I know."

I felt so lost in these moments. I was nine, and I was on the kitchen floor, comforting my mother as she contemplated suicide. Sometimes my sister or brother would be around during these moments, and it would be all of us holding our mother and trying to say the right things but feeling in over our heads. But it was the worst when it was just Mom and I. I didn't know what to say or what to do, so I just held her. And once it was all done, she'd say, "I'm fine. I'm fine."

She said that a lot actually, almost like a mantra. She was speaking to me, but it felt like she was saying it to herself. She'd get up from the kitchen floor and go to bed, and I'd sit at the small desk in my room, alone, and cry.

And that same pit I felt in my stomach when Dad was high, I felt it again in moments like this, when I comforted my mom because she felt broken and alone.

Looking back, it's clear to me that she was struggling with a deep depression in the shadow of a very messy divorce, and yet she never spoke of her mental health. She never discussed seeking help to process what she was feeling. She never even used words like *depression* or *anxiety* or any variation of them. The closest she got was when she announced that she was going to kill herself. But it was unlikely that she could afford to seek out help. We were already getting help from the church for groceries and other necessities, and accepting that help really went against Mom's values. She mentioned that a lot—how much shame she felt getting help from the church or the government. "I just can't let myself be a welfare case," she'd say.

The few times we did visit the bishop's storehouse, a grocery outlet funded by the Mormon church, Mom silently looked at the shelves, took what we needed, her face pale, hands shaking, lips in a flat line, shoulders slumped. Everything about her screamed shame. We'd arrive home, and once the things were put away, she'd sit in her room and cry until she fell asleep—but regardless of how many times I asked her what was wrong, she'd always say, "I'm fine. I'm just fine." And as she said it, I could see tears welling up in her eyes.

When friends from church, aunts and uncles, coworkers asked how she was doing, she said the same thing: "I'm fine. I'm fine." Every once in a while, someone would push a little, tell her they were worried about her, but she always stuck to her story—"I'm fine. I'm just fine." Then she'd stretch a forced smile across her lips, and close the conversation with, "I'm working through it." But her moist eyes, her slumped shoulders—everything about her—said otherwise.

At the time, I didn't have language to articulate what she was suffering from. I only knew that my mother was deeply sad. And looking back, it seems clear that others knew it too. But admitting to that sadness was something she refused to do openly.

Her silence, her unwillingness to discuss what

she was really feeling, showed me, as a young man, that when it came to depression, anxiety, stress—all of it—I was to adhere to a code of silence. I was to deny how I was feeling if it came up, even if I was obviously suffering. I was to keep my emotions to myself and never confide in anyone about them. I was to say I was fine, even if being "fine" felt like a far-off swath of land in a very different universe.

Less than a year after Dad left, he invited his mistress to work as his secretary in the backyard.

He gave her a nice desk in the back of the shop, and she sat there, typing away, filing paperwork, and answering calls with a chipper waitress–style laughter I could hear every time I stepped into the backyard.

I was young and Mormon, and I'd never seen two people open-mouth kiss before, except on TV, until Dad started making out with his girlfriend in his pickup parked in the backyard. She must have been close to 10 years younger than he was. She had bell-shaped hips, a slender waist, and long, very curly black hair. She wore a gold cross around her neck and so much perfume I could smell it when I played on the trampoline.

When they kissed, it was all tongue, and it was grabby, and I remember sitting on our trampoline as a child, just watching it happen, wondering who the heck this man was and what he'd done with my father. And I must say, once his new girlfriend started making appearances in the backyard, on the whole he appeared incredibly confident about all of it. No shame whatsoever. It was almost a cockof-the-walk kind of confidence. I can't remember Dad ever strutting before, but once she took the job as his secretary, he started walking with this hip-swinging swagger, the right side of his lip curled a little, all of it giving off a Billy Idol feel.

He abandoned the first couple buttons on his shirt and he got himself a gold necklace. He'd always worn cologne, but it seemed like he was bathing in it now. It was like there was a cloud of man musk just above his head, and I felt confident that people behind him at stoplights could probably smell it. He'd somehow changed from a pretty buttoned-down, hardworking Mormon father to a cross between a sleazy car salesman and a Texas pimp.

He fixed his hair a lot in the reflection of the pickup's mirrors. He was all smiles, almost like getting kissy-face with a new woman in view of his family was something to be proud of. And let me just say, it wasn't. At least not to me. And I know my mother struggled with it too. Dad was literally rubbing our noses in it, and he held this disposition that he was absolutely thrilled to be brandishing his new life in front of his soon-to-be ex-wife and children each and every workday.

He also seemed to be spending an incredible amount of money: a custom paint job on his work truck and new tools, many of them huge and specialized ones that needed to be brought into the shop with a forklift. It was a daily thing, really. He also started hiring new employees. Before the separation, I think he had two people working for him in that shop. But in the months that followed his leaving, his crew more than doubled, with six employees (not including his secretary), and suddenly the backyard looked more and more like a flourishing, successful business. And he seemed to be spending a lot of money on his new girlfriend—jewelry, clothes, the works—as my mother slaved away working days, evenings, and weekends to make ends meet.

It was just after school one afternoon when Dad first introduced me to his new girlfriend. My brother and I were in the backyard, and Dad called our names for what felt like the first time in a long time. We walked across the yard together cautiously, not sure what to expect, and he said with a puffed-out chest, "I want you to meet my new friend." And while he said *friend* with a devil's grin, Trent and I shared a sideways glance, because we knew she was more than a friend.

She crouched down and smiled at both of us. She told us that she had boys close to our ages and she hoped we could become friends with them. She wore far more makeup than I was used to. The smell of her perfume was almost overwhelming. Her smile was wide, her teeth straight but stained from coffee, and she had a gold cap on one of her front teeth. She wore a dark maroon shirt and black jeans that matched her dark hair and eyes. Her dark brown cowboy boots matched my father's, and I realized they must have been a gift.

I looked at this woman and felt like she was

an outsider. She didn't belong in my family, and that made her presence overwhelming. But what shook me the most was when Dad said, "Someday I'm hoping you boys can call her Mom. Won't that be something special? To have two moms?" She stood and smiled at Dad, and he winked, and I had this strong urge to run away—to flee, to hide. I didn't want anything to do with her, or their relationship, or this new life I'd been presented with. And in the days to follow, I tried actively to avoid her because her simple presence made me feel a tightness in my stomach that I didn't understand. Looking back now, I realize that what I was struggling with was change. Her presence represented a rift, a change in my family, that I wasn't ready to accept and didn't understand, so I made it a point to avoid her as much as possible as a way to gain control.

All of it was a confusing mess of separation and togetherness that created a tightness in my abdomen very similar to the butterflies I experienced on roller coasters. I was afraid of my mother, never knowing when she'd blow up, or when she'd begin to cry, or when she'd tell me she wanted to end her life. I didn't trust my father because I didn't know what to expect from him or who he might be from one minute to the next. The state of being afraid is what I remember most during this time and all of it sat deep in my gut, like a seed, germinating what would later become a lifelong struggle with anxiety.

But as a child, I assumed I had a sick stomach,

so I drank Pepto-Bismol. Lots of it. Almost a bottle a week. And when that ran out, I drank Mylanta, that white, chalky, mint-flavored crap people take for heartburn. I walked around the house with the open bottle like it was no big thing, like I was some middle-aged drunk in a robe nursing a hangover instead of a ten-year-old boy establishing an anxiety disorder.

But with all the chaos going on in my family, no one seemed to think I was acting all that strange. I stayed home from school at least once a week because of anxiety-related stomach pains and watched TV shows from the '60s and '70s. I found so much comfort in those golden-era shows. I wanted my parents to be like Ricky and Lucy. I wished they could argue, but in a comical way followed by a resolution, instead of my mother telling my father in the backyard that she might as well kill herself and my father replying in a drunken slur, "You've been saying that for years, darling. When ya gonna take that check to the bank?" Only for my mother to say, "I wish you'd pay child support, so I had some checks to take to the bank."

And round and round they'd go, until I was nursing an empty bottle of Pepto.

During the separation, Mom would sometimes cross the yard and walk into Dad's shop and scream at him over something that happened in the divorce proceedings, something I didn't under-stand. I could feel the betrayal and frustration steaming off her. Sometimes she'd scream at his mistress, calling her a slut, a home-wrecker, and a number of other names I knew I wasn't allowed to say at my age. And she'd scream back, telling Mom to get a life, to get over it.

And my mother would say, "How can I get a life when you are always in my backyard?"

Sometimes she just went over there and cried.

Sometimes she sat on her bed and looked out the back window at his new life.

During one of my parents' arguments, Mom screamed at Dad, her face a hot mess of angry tears, her right hand coming down like a karate chop pointed at his chest. She was pleading with him to pay child support. She mentioned the new tools and all the deliveries, and he looked over her shoulder, to see me watching from the trampoline.

"You need to stop telling lies. I've been paying you," he said in this calm, slick tone, his eyes glancing at her and then at me.

We made eye contact, and he winked.

He held pretty hard to that story. I once confronted him in the backyard about not paying child support. He pulled me into his shop and then motioned me into the office with a wave of his hand. He sat down at his desk and pulled out a black binder. In it were pages of xeroxed checks made out to my mother. "See?" he asked. He tapped the pages, and my mouth dropped. It felt like I'd just entered a true-crime story, or like I was the omnipotent narrator in my own book—suddenly I'd seen through the mist and it all became clear, and Dad was the one I could trust, not Mom.

"I'll bet your mom is spending that money on

herself," he said, looking me straight in the face.

Then he looked at his new girlfriend through the open office door. And this time, he gave her the wink.

I totally bought it.

Hook, line, and sinker.

I confronted Mom about those checks later, and she closed her eyes, took a deep breath, feeling yet another betrayal from my dad. She told me he pulled out that same binder in front of the lawyers, and after many days of back-and-forth and calls to both banks, it was determined that he was writing checks, making copies of them to put in that binder, and then throwing the originals in the garbage. Which, I would like to say, has to be one of the lowest moves I've ever seen. And yet none of these revelations made me feel any better.

I felt caught in the middle of it all, both physically and emotionally: physically because these arguments were happening in my backyard and emotionally because of tug-of-war moments like the child support checks.

That night, when Mom told me what had happened at court, I woke in the middle of the night and threw up from anxiety. For the first time since Dad left, I felt like I'd been wronged. I felt like my father had cheated me, my mother, my family. I sat on the bathroom linoleum, my back against the tub, everyone asleep, and felt this surge of anger at my father for the first time. The next Sunday, when no one was in the shop, I grabbed my slingshot from my dresser and I marched into the backyard.

I broke a hole in every window in my dad's shop. Every single one.

The next week I waited for my father to confront me about what I'd done. To come to the house for the first time in months, knock on the door, and give me a good lecture. Maybe tell me I had to work in his shop to pay for the broken glass. Anything. But it never happened. He never asked me any questions about breaking his windows. In many ways I wish he had, because I could have told him why I did it and maybe it would have caused us to talk, and then maybe he would have paid child support, and then maybe my mother might not have had to work so much, and then maybe she wouldn't have been so depressed and wouldn't have talked so much about ending her life.

But nada, nothing. And that lack of reaction felt far worse than getting in trouble, because I realized there was nothing I could do to change the situation. And that realization meant that I had no choice but to continue to wade through my father's lies and my mother's raw anger and depression, and all of that felt like I was in this bubbling pot of hot water—and all I wanted to do was get out of that pot, but I couldn't, so I just drank my Pepto.

One evening, my parents began arguing in the yard. Dad was obviously high, his red-and-brown plaid polyester shirt half untucked, the top two buttons open, his gold chain reflecting in the Utah sun. His legs were unsteady as he stared at his soon-to-be ex-wife with glossy eyes, a twisted half grin on his face, like he was finally free of her and he could say and do what he wanted. He was ready to give her a real zinger—I could see it in his face—but he was too high to say anything overly brilliant, so he just stood there and smiled as she screamed.

But the moment she broke for a breath, he had the audacity to accuse her of being crazy. "You need help," he said, pointing at her with a lazy, calloused index finger. "I don't think you're right in the head." That last line came out with a sloppy twang, and then he tapped the side of his temple and that motion caused him to lose his balance and fall onto the grass. He finished his declaration in a seated position. "You. Need. Help."

"*I'm* crazy?" Mom said. "*I'm* crazy? Look at you! *You* need help. You can't even stand up!"

They went back and forth like that for a while, both of them calling the other crazy, while I just sat on our trampoline wearing greasy sweatpants and a black *Teenage Mutant Ninja Turtles* T-shirt that read "Cowabunga, Dude," my hair a mess, an open bottle of Pepto in my right hand, feeling like the manager of a psychiatric hospital.

Within a year of the separation, a fence was built between his end of the yard and ours.

But the question for me is, Who built it? In my memories, it was my father. I can see him building it. I can see him pounding in the nails, sweat dripping from his face and along the back of his polyester western-style shirts, a leather tool belt around his waist. And for years, I assumed he built it because he was tired of Mom walking across the yard and giving him and his new girlfriend a piece of her mind. Years later, I even had an essay about it published in a literary journal. But when I asked my mom about it in my late twenties, she told me it was my grandfather who built it. She said it was because Grandpa was ashamed of what Dad was doing. When I asked my older half-brother about the fence, he said it had something to do with Grandpa still owning the property my dad's shop was on, and he needed a barrier to keep from losing the land in the divorce.

Regardless of who built the stupid thing, the fact remains that there was a solid cedar fence separating my dad's side of the yard and my mother's. There was a second gravel driveway laid so my dad could go to work without using the family driveway, and it was sandwiched between two barbed wire fences. The cedar fence must have been at least seven feet tall, because no adult on either side could see over it, even if they stood on their toes. There were no gaps in the fence, no gate, just a couple knotholes my brother and I sometimes peeked through. If I got on the trampoline and jumped a couple times, I could see Dad's side of the yard in flashes.

On the east and west sides of the wooden fence was barbed wire to keep Grandpa's cows in their pasture, and I can remember my father yelling at my mom from his side of the fence, "Good fences make good neighbors!"

She informed him, from her side of the fence, that they both still owned the land and she could cross the fence anytime she felt inclined.

"I don't see a gate in here," he said. "Good luck climbing this fence!"

All of it felt like an episode of *I Love Lucy* playing out in real life, but no one was laughing—especially me. The really tragic part was that while this fence separated my parents, which was sorely needed, it also shut me out from my dad almost completely. I couldn't climb his fence either. And that separation, that void of not being able to at least see him during his good days, left me feeling incredibly lost. And sure, once a month we were supposed to spend a weekend with him, but the sad thing is I can't remember him ever taking us to his home. I didn't know where he was living at this time.

Sometimes, though, he'd pick my brother and me up, and we'd climb in his truck, our bags packed for the weekend. We'd go to McDonald's, get a Happy Meal in the drive-through, and then he'd take us back home. We'd hardly speak, and then in the driveway he'd say, "Sorry, boys. I just don't have the time this weekend." Then he'd back out of the family driveway, pull into his driveway, and go to work in the backyard. My brother and I, we'd be left to sit there, eating our chicken nuggets and fries on the front porch steps, listening to Dad's country music on the shop stereo as he worked. His girlfriend would eventually pull in, and they'd laugh and joke, and we'd just sit there, listening, feeling like the third wheels on their date.

It was like he was living so close I could almost touch him, but he wasn't there anymore, and I didn't know how to manage that absence.

And all of this—my dad not being an active father, his not paying child support, the lies— pushed my mom deeper into a spiral of depression and endless work hours.

Her work hours peaked at Christmastime. Mom worked days at Provo Power, evenings cleaning houses, and weekends at a music store. At nine or ten o'clock at night she'd arrive home wearing paint-stained sweatpants and an old faded T-shirt, a plastic bucket filled with yellow rubber gloves, toothbrushes, Lysol, and a scrubbing brush in her right hand. She'd drop the bucket, her fingertips wrinkled from washing floors. Then she would step into the garage and return a moment later with the navy blue dress she wore to her office job at Provo Power slung over her forearm.

Then she'd ask me about homework and chores, and I would have done none of them. And sure, so much of this was my being a lazy young man who was left alone most days. But more than anything, I was scared, and depressed, and lonely, and I needed someone to tell me everything was going to be okay. I needed someone to tell me this fear I felt in my gut, the throwing up, the anxiety, was something I could learn to live with. I needed someone to hold me. I needed someone to talk to.

But Mom didn't have time for those things, because she was trying to provide for a family while paying legal fees for what seemed like an endless divorce and paying off my father's debts. I didn't know how to tell her how I was feeling because I simply couldn't make sense of it. I was ten by this point, and daily I thought about suicide, same as Mom.

I think Mom just wanted me to do what was expected of me—homework, chores, the basics—because she had so much going on, and the last thing she needed was to come home to some unmotivated and depressed ten-year-old. I was literally the last thing she had to deal with at the end of the day, and after she'd worked all-consuming hours, day in and day out, I was the straw that broke the camel's back.

All of this tension came out in late-night moments when Mom yelled at me about homework and chores until we were both crying. Then she'd go in her room and lock the door, and I'd go to my bedroom and sit in the closet, both of us unable to communicate, unable to express our fears and frustrations and overwhelming feelings that weren't our faults but simply our reactions to a very hard situation.

And when things got really bad, when my fear was too much and I was numb all over, I went to my grandparents' house. I spent quite a bit of time there, actually. They were my dad's parents, and it was their beef farm that bordered our property.

Their house was less than a mile from ours if I walked along the street. It was even closer if I cut through their field, being careful not to step in any manure. They were both farmers, and had been as long as they'd been alive. Or at least, that's what

I assumed. I didn't know all that much about their lives before I came along—and to be honest, as a kid, I probably didn't really care. I was interested in the here and now, and the way they hugged me when I arrived and before I left, and how they filled my tummy with an almost shameful amount of candy every time I stopped by.

But the candy, the hugs, all of that suddenly became secondary in my hierarchy of reasons to visit my grandparents after Dad left. I remember friends telling me fond stories about visiting their grandparents: how they got spoiled, and how the rules flexed, and all that other stuff kids look forward to. And sure, before Dad left, I looked forward to that sort of stuff too. But after Dad left, visiting my grandparents became more akin to therapy. Their house was quiet. It was always the same, making it predictable in a way I craved. There was a calmness inside their walls, a simple peace that was addictive to me as a child. I could go there and just sit and breathe, almost like I'd found the eye of a hurricane. I spent many hours there. I knew where they hid the key in the small flower pot next to the door. In many ways, their home became my safe place.

I remember the first Christmas without Dad. Below the tree were as many gifts as the year before. I received pants, shirts, and socks, but I didn't care about those. I cared about toys. My stockings were filled with candy and toy cars. But the huge, exciting gift for me at the time was a Wrestling Buddy: a canvas pillow shaped like

The Ultimate Warrior. Man, I beat the crap out of that thing on our trampoline.

Looking back on the hardships of that Christmas, I acknowledge that Mom would have been justified in giving us half as much, or nothing at all. Although I should have, I cannot recall wanting for anything other than my father that year.

As I searched through the gifts, I kept expecting to see packages marked "From Dad." But I never did. I thought about that, and about how much I missed dragging Dad out of bed early on Christmas morning to open gifts. I longed for him to be sitting on the sofa at 6:00 a.m., holding a can of Pepsi and watching us tear wrapping paper. I missed the remarks he used to make: "Oh, that's a cool robot," or "We didn't have stuff like that when I was a boy. You are one lucky guy." All while holding a garbage sack, insisting that we bring him the paper as soon as we finished opening the gift, and not letting us leave to play with our new toys without giving him a hug.

I don't know how Mom afforded Christmas without Dad's income. But she managed. When I think about Mom's long hours, I cannot help but be grateful that she considered how important Christmas was when you're a kid.

Late on Christmas afternoon, Dad visited his shop. Trent said, "I hope he stops by."

The truck started, and we ran to the kitchen window. He drove across the gravel lane, heading toward Center Street, his right hand resting lazily on the wheel, his gaze set forward. Trent and I ran from the house and stood between the gravel lane and the road. Trent raised his hand—his flattop must have been barely visible above the hood of Dad's truck. Dad's face was expressionless. It was like nothing was behind his eyes—no emotion, no excitement, nothing.

He was on painkillers.

It was twenty degrees. Neither Trent nor I were wearing coats. I wasn't wearing shoes.

Dad didn't leap from his pickup, put his arms around us, and draw our faces against his chest, like he did just one year earlier. He didn't look into my eyes, drag his warm hand across my cold cheek, and say, "Merry Christmas." And he didn't pull gift after gift from the passenger seat, tell us how much he missed us, and promise that we would spend more time together.

Dad stopped the truck with a jerk, and the tires skidded in the gravel. He stepped from the pickup and stumbled a bit as he attempted to get his footing in the gravel. He licked his lips and straightened his shirt. The truck's cab light shined on his face, and I could see his eyes, his dark, wide pupils. He reached into his jeans, fumbled in his leather wallet, his legs unsteady, and handed us each a twenty-dollar bill. "Merry Christmas," he said. "Now get in the house before you freeze to death." He climbed back into his truck. Trent and I stood there for a bit, holding our money, until Dad honked the horn and made a shooing motion with his hand.

We walked into the house as Dad drove away.

As a ten-year-old, I felt like twenty dollars was a substantial amount of money. I must admit, I was exhilarated, like he'd handed me hundreds of dollars. As an adult, I sometimes think about Mom's long hours and the thought she put into each gift. Then I think about the twenty dollars Dad grudgingly pulled from his wallet, and it seems meaningless. Mom must've known this, and it must have broken her heart to see Trent and I wave the bills in her face, both of us above the moon over his thoughtless gift.

"That was very nice of him," she said and turned away.

I don't know how long the fence stood. It was at least a year. Dad kept working in the backyard. And then one day, he moved his shop, and I don't know if I've ever gotten a straight answer as to why it happened. I heard there were noise complaints from neighbors, which caused the city to reexamine his business license. But that all seemed strange to me considering we had only one neighbor close enough to hear my dad banging on sheet metal. But years later I heard a rumor that it was Mom who called the city and made the complaints, posing as neighbors. I don't know if this is true, but in many ways I hope it is, because that would have been pretty tough of her.

I remember Dad hauling his equipment away, and once he was gone, Mom told me she now owned his shop. She said she was going to begin renting it out, so we needed to tear down the fence

ANXIOUSLY EVER AFTER

and "burn it."

It was the "burn it" part that stood out. She said it with fire in her eyes, her right hand slightly shaking, almost like this is what she'd longed to do from the moment it went up.

She started small, burning a few desiccated weeds with half a dozen fence panels and a few broken pallets on weekend nights. Camp-sized fires gradually grew to bonfires. Flames reached higher, stretching to twenty feet. Gray smoke engulfed the house, and each weekend my clothing smelled of sweet burning branches. Everything my dad left behind she lit on fire. But it felt like more than just cleaning up the property so someone could rent the shop.

It felt like a cleansing.

It felt like we were burning memories.

Burning the reminders of Dad.

She burned his fence and she burned his junk. She burned clothing he left behind, the boots and work shirts and coveralls. She burned the paperwork he left in the house and in the office. She burned old pallets, pictures, cardboard, Styrofoam packaging, PVC pipes, random piles of lumber, tools. If it could burn, and it was once my dad's, it went in the fire. Every weekend there was a fire in our yard. And once it was all gone, the only thing left was the clubhouse.

I must say, building that clubhouse was one of the warmest memories I have of my father. Dad hunched over me, smelling like sweat and sawdust, as I crouched over a strip of lumber. With his left hand, knuckles scarred, he helped me hold a nail. With his right, he helped me swing the hammer. "Get it started," he said, "so it'll stay in place."

Together we tapped the nail, and then drove it home.

We banged our hammers, and the sound seemed to travel a great distance along the valley. I held nails between my lips, like Dad did. Sometimes he placed his hands on his hips, and gazed at the plans he'd drawn on a yellow pad of paper, his face rich with thought. We constructed the clubhouse on a Saturday morning.

It wasn't anything special, I admit. The club- house was more or less a large cedar box resting on the ground, mostly made from two-by-fours and fencing slats. It was probably six feet high, five feet wide, and ten feet deep. It had a dirt floor, a low ceiling, a north-facing door, and a west-facing window. But I didn't see the simplicity of it. At the time, it felt like a huge accomplishment. A great structure built by many men.

But now, in the shadow of the smoke from our weekend fires, the clubhouse looked faded, and it leaned slightly to one side. It's not that I didn't want to play in it anymore. I did, actually. But it had been on Dad's side of the property, and I couldn't access it because of the fence. As I looked at the ash piles, that clubhouse really was the final reminder of Dad on the property.

Mom looked at the clubhouse, her eyes dry, the tips of her bleached-blond hair singed and the roots coming in black, and said, "We can't have that" while pointing at the clubhouse. "We just can't. You kids don't play there anymore," she said. "Look at this dump." Mom placed her hands on her hips. "We should burn it down." She raised and dropped her palm with force. "Right to the ground."

That afternoon, she filled the clubhouse with balls of crumpled newspaper and soaked it in ten gallons of gasoline. Then she gave me the garden hose, turned it on high, and told me, "If this gets out of hand, put it out."

It was a scene I'll never forget. Mom in knee-length jean shorts and an old green B.U.M. brand T-shirt, hunching down on one knee next to the old clubhouse.

I stood to the side, in baggy black-and-gray striped MC Hammer pants, white and purple Reebok Pump shoes, and a black T-shirt with Bart Simpson on it. I had buckteeth and freckles, my hair was mashed on one side from sleep, and between my teeth were the crumbs of a Pop-Tart. I was far from being responsible enough to put out a fire, and yet there I was, ready for anything.

Just before Mom clicked the lighter, I asked, "Are you sure this is a good idea?"

She looked up at me, one knee still bent, and gave me those hard eyes moms often get, the same ones she gave me when I announced that I could live on my own after learning how to microwave soup. Honestly, I couldn't understand how she thought lighting our clubhouse on fire was a good idea. But I was the kid and she was the parent, so I just stood there with the garden hose.

She clicked our long-nosed, red-handled barbecue lighter at the base of the clubhouse, and the flames inhaled, rapidly coating the clubhouse. She sprang back and fell into a sitting position on the gravel. Then she rolled to her hands and knees and ran toward the shop. The heat hit me in seconds and the fire stretched high above us, licking the power lines that fed the shop.

I remember thinking how cool this all was for a short moment. I mean, I was a young boy, and fire was always awesome. But then I looked at the garden hose in my hand and couldn't help but feel underqualified to be on fire duty, and all of it filled my body with an overwhelming pins-and-needles dread.

But the scariest part wasn't the fire.

It was Mom laughing as it burned. It was jolly, crazy, hunched-over laughing at first. She clapped her hands and then covered her mouth and laughed, nearly in tears. Then, as the flames went higher, the laughter settled into more of a giggle, the kind you might make when things are finally working out and life is finally starting to go your way. It was the kind of laughter you make when you are hit with relief, because you don't have to worry about something anymore. I hadn't seen my mother laugh in months, and yet there she was, standing next to 25-foot flames, laughing while I stood holding a garden hose, feeling absolute terror.

All I could think about was months earlier, when my father called her crazy. And sure, there are moments of temporary madness. And there was no doubt that my mother was experiencing one of those moments. But even as a young child, I wondered how much of her was inside of me, and for the first time I felt a very real fear that my mother was, in fact, mad.

But I don't think the madness of the situation fully dawned on Mom until our only neighbor within a stone's throw opened his second-story window and asked if he should call the fire department.

"No!" Mom said in a rushed, assertive voice. "It's all under control. We're just"—she sheepishly kicked some dirt—"getting rid of the clubhouse. See? Clint's got the hose."

She shrugged like it was just another thing, as she stood next to an inferno. Then our neighbor looked at me, and I held up the garden hose and gave him this awkward "I'm as nervous about this as you" thumbs-up and half grin.

The neighbor looked at me again, then at my mother, and then at the fire whose flames were reaching over his head as he stood on the second floor of his home. I thought for sure he was going to call 911, but he didn't. He just shook his head in that small-town "I'm not getting involved" sort of way and shut his window.

The fire, my life, all of it was out of control, and this was the first time I can remember having a panic attack. I was absolutely terrified. But I didn't have the language for it. I didn't know what to make of the tightness in my stomach, or the way my hands shook because they were numb, or how fast my heart was beating, or the way my thoughts raced inside my head like a rat trying to find its way out of my skull, or the hot waves that went up and down my body that were somehow hotter than the fire raging in front of me.

There's this famous meme of a dog sitting in a burning room, with the caption "It's fine." When I think back on my mother burning down the clubhouse, it feels a lot like I was living that meme.

This was the first time I knew, without a doubt, that I couldn't live with my mother anymore.

WHERE DAD LIVED

A little more than a year after Dad left the back-yard shop, he kind of disappeared. It was hard to explain to friends and family that I really had no idea where my father lived. I mean, we used to know where he lived. He had this new shop, with a house attached, on the east side of Provo—probably five or six miles across town. With enough gumption, I could ride my bike over there, but it was a long haul for a kid. Dad occasionally picked me up for a weekend, but he was inconsistent. He still regularly pulled the McDonald's Happy Meal move, and then he'd take me back home and I'd quietly unpack my things. And in moments like that, I felt like he was a huge jerk. And after more than a year of this, I stopped trusting that he was going to be a consistent part of my life, so I gave up on trying to visit him.

I felt like I was doing all the work to maintain the relationship, and I remember thinking, *The ball is in your hands, old man. If you want to be my dad, you're going to have to call me.* And part of me really, honestly hoped that he'd start reaching out. But he didn't, and by the time I turned twelve, he moved from that house with the shop on the east side of town, but he never told me he was moving, and I'm not sure how long he'd been gone before I noticed. One day I rode my bike to his home, knocked on the door, and discovered that new people lived there.

Which is kind of sad, honestly.

At one point he told me he'd married the woman he left my mother for, but I didn't go to the wedding or anything. I wasn't invited, so I didn't really know. I knew they'd been living together. He'd been missing from my life for about a year, and during that time I watched the original *Star Wars* trilogy on VHS at least once a week. At the time, I couldn't understand what attracted me so much to the story of Luke and his father, Darth Vader. But now, when I look back at this time, how could I not be attracted to that story? How could any child living through the abandonment of their own father not long for a moment similar to the one at the end of *Return of the Jedi*, when Luke takes off Darth Vader's black mask to finally see the heavily scarred but ultimately loving and very human face of Anakin Skywalker, so that his father can utter a phrase I longed for my father to say someday: "You were right. You were right about me"?

No child wants to give up on the hope that their father is redeemable and that he will one day change and come back to them and be the father they long for—or in my case, the father I had before the night Dad left.

By the time I was thirteen, I couldn't recall the last time I'd seen Dad. Then one afternoon, my older brother came into my bedroom and said, "I found him."

"Found who?" I asked.

"Dad."

Trent was a long, slender kid now, with glasses like Dad and his dirty-blond hair in bowl cut, parted to the side. He was my only full-blood sibling, and at the time, we were close. He was the kind of kid who got really excited about computers and *Star Trek*, and—I'm not lying here—he actually tried to learn Klingon. He was the kid that took electronics apart and put them back together. But at the same time, he was a pretty stereotypical nerd, with a lot of other nerdy friends who also spoke Klingon and smelled a lot like mustard because none of them were huge on personal hygiene. On the whole, though, he was a good big brother, who would drive me to meet with friends. And after Dad left, Trent taught me how to tie a tie, and shave the stubble along my chin, and mow the lawn.

But the moment he told me about Dad, he didn't say it with excitement, or shock, or anything like that. He said it like he'd found a lost toy or article of clothing that he hadn't put any real effort into finding. And yet I was curious as to what Dad had been up to, where he was living, and I felt this glimmer of hope when Trent told me he'd found Dad. I wondered if maybe he'd taken this time to sort things out—just maybe, he might want to be my dad again.

Trent never told me how he discovered where Dad lived. Or if he did, I don't remember the details.

Trent was sixteen and owned a 1980-something gray four-door Chrysler that Grandma helped him buy. We drove twenty minutes south on Interstate 15, to Mapleton. Dad's Ford pickup was in the driveway. The brake lights were on.

Trent and I went to the door, rang the bell, waited a moment, and then knocked. No one answered. I looked through the windows, and on the coffee table there was a picture of Dad smiling, with his arm around his new wife, so I knew it was his place. The door was unlocked, so I went in. Paintings of Catholic saints and crosses hung from the walls and the house smelled of turned milk, beer, and scented candles. I wandered the house. In the kitchen, on a dining room chair, was one of Dad's western shirts. I sat on the living room sofa with the intention of waiting for Dad to come home. I didn't know if I was going to ask him where he'd been, or just jump out at him and give him a "Surprise!" sort of thing, almost like we'd been playing this very long game of hide-and-seek. Part of me, the pissed off part, the bold and angry part, wanted to know why he had moved without telling me.

Trent was in the front yard next to the pickup.

He called me outside. His voice was high and shaky, and when I went outside, Trent's eyes were wide, his face flushed, hands trembling.

Hunched over in the truck was Dad. His leather boot was wedged on the brake, and thick white sludge filled the corners of his mouth. Trent opened the truck door and I could hear the gurgling of

Dad's slow, irregular breaths. It sounded like he was choking, but somehow I knew that wasn't the problem; nonetheless, I didn't know what was wrong with him.

But that sound, that gasping-for-air sound, almost like he was drowning. The wet scraping sounds from his very dry mouth. The strain of his lungs, his body jerking with each breath. I can hear it, even now, as I type this almost 25 years later. It still makes me tremble. I'd never felt fear like that. Not when Mom burned down the clubhouse. Not when Dad walked out of our lives and I was uncertain of my future.

I had no comparison or language for the dread of hearing my father struggle for breath, and I remember not fully understanding the situation but feeling confident that Dad was going to die. I could see it in his pale face, and his dry lips, and the way his body was twisted, and contorted, and limp, and on its side, in what seemed like the most uncomfortable position imaginable. I could hear it in his gasps for air. I could smell it in the sweat that ran along his chest and neck and scalp.

I shook Dad's leg and he inhaled with a snarl, sat up, looked at me, looked at my brother, and then closed his eyes and fell to his side again.

"What's wrong with him?" I asked.

Trent didn't say anything for a while, but I could tell by the way his eyes searched Dad's body that he was also terrified.

"We need to get him in the house," Trent said.

Together, we grabbed Dad's left arm and tugged. He smelled like BO and dust and sheet metal, his body unusually hot from being hunched over in the truck's cab with the windows up in 90-degree heat. We got him upright but not out of the truck, and as we did, Dad's boot came off the brake and the truck rolled backward into the road.

I jumped out of the way, and Trent ran alongside the truck and stomped on the emergency brake. The pickup stopped with a jerk, the bed of it a few feet into the road, and Dad slammed his face into the horn. The sound made him inhale and growl and open his eyes again; his pupils were wide and dark. He leaned to the left and spilled into the driveway, landing on his left shoulder, legs and arms spread wide, his butt in the air. His square-framed glasses slid from his face, cracked on the asphalt, and bounced into the grass.

He was unconscious again with his face on the asphalt.

Trent tugged Dad to a sitting position, crouched down, and tried to lift him.

"Help me," Trent said.

I put Dad's right arm over my neck, and Trent did the same with his left arm, and together we tugged Dad's limp body into the house; his boot tips scraped across the driveway. We set him on the couch and I told Trent I was going to call an ambulance.

Dad woke suddenly and said in this sloppy, confused, half-awake slur, "Stop. No. I just fine. Don't call nobody." His left hand waved limply, like he was trying to reach out and grab me by the shirt collar, but he couldn't muster the balance to stand.

He eventually went to sleep again, and within a few moments, an ambulance arrived and Trent and I followed it to the hospital in Payson, Utah. We sat next to Dad as he lay sprawled on the gurney in a blue and white hospital gown. His breathing was irregular next to the consistent beeps and pings of the hospital machines, but it was far steadier than what it had been a few hours earlier as he gasped for air in his pickup truck. Sometimes Dad would open his eyes and roll them in circles and then shut them again. A doctor entered the room. She was a middle-aged woman with black hair and eyes, and she was wearing a lab coat. I asked what was wrong with Dad.

"He overdosed, but we're not sure on what just yet. An opioid of some kind." She said it flatly in a clinical tone, her face in a clipboard. Then she looked up at these two young boys, alone, not an adult in sight, and changed to a more appropriate bedside tone. "He's going to be okay. But it was a close one." She paused for a moment. She asked us what happened, and we told her how we found him hunched over in his truck, alone.

She looked at the clipboard again, then at us, and said, "You probably saved his life."

She gave us a half smile, and I had the hardest time feeling proud of myself. I didn't feel relief, like I'd saved a life, or even my *father's* life. I felt an emotion I can only describe as a hot flash of fear. It started in my stomach and then trickled into my hands and feet. I wanted to run out of that hospital. I wanted to be anywhere but where I was—yet I just stood, motionless.

She asked us some more questions about Dad and what he might have taken. But we really didn't have any answers, because this was the first time we'd seen him in a very long time. And when I look back on this moment, I realize I probably should have drawn more conclusions. I should have figured out that Dad was struggling with addiction, but at the time, I was just a scared little Mormon boy, being faced with words I didn't understand. I didn't really know what *overdose* meant. I didn't know this was a sign that Dad might be addicted to painkillers, and I don't think Trent understood any of that either. So the doctor spoke, and we nodded, acting like we understood, but really we had no idea. Our dad was in the hospital, he was sick, and he almost died. That much we knew, and that was enough to make me so afraid and overwhelmed that anything else, any other information, went right through me. I stood in that hospital room, next to my father and across from my brother, in the throes of a full-blown panic attack and feeling more alone and lost than I'd ever felt in my life.

In my memory, he was released the same day. But that doesn't seem right to me now. It seems odd that he would be released the same day after an overdose, but I could be mistaken. Perhaps it was a day or two later. What I do remember very clearly was taking Dad home from the hospital. It was late. It was dark out.

He didn't say a word as the nurse helped him to a wheelchair and then pushed him to the street corner. I walked next to Dad and studied the way he drew in his cheeks and puckered his lips. The way his knees fell to the sides. I couldn't decide if he was angry or embarrassed. Perhaps he was just trying to look tough. I didn't know.

Trent and I took Dad home. Dad looked out the window, Trent looked at the road, and I looked at Dad from the back seat. It was silent most of the drive except for the few times when Dad said, "Turn here."

We pulled into Dad's driveway and he didn't say thanks for driving him home, or for taking him to the hospital, or for saving his life. And he didn't ask how we found him, nor did he explain why he didn't make contact with us for a year or say that we could come back and visit sometime.

"She's leaving me," he said. I could hear the scrape of his damaged right hand rubbing the whiskers along his jaw. He didn't tell us why she was leaving, or how long she'd been gone. I eventually heard a rumor that she'd cheated on him, same as he'd cheated on my mother.

"It's late," he said. "I didn't want you to see me like that. Please go home." Dad stepped from the car and with slow, heavy steps walked into the house.

Trent and I drove home, and that night, I didn't sleep. I couldn't possibly. I went to bed, sure. But I just lay there, knots in my stomach, playing the scene of what happened with Dad over and over again in my mind, it turning and bubbling, round and round. Later in life, I would discover that these thoughts, these emotions, the flush of anxiety I had while thinking about what I'd just experienced, are called ruminating thoughts. They are something anxiety sufferers often live with, but I didn't have a name for them. I didn't know why I couldn't stop thinking about the experience. I contemplated waking my mother. Maybe tell her what happened just to have someone, anyone, to talk to about my father's overdose. But I didn't know how she'd react, and part of me worried it might send her deeper into depression, so I didn't say a word. I didn't tell anyone about it—family or friends. I just stayed in bed, feeling alone and scared. About 7:00 a.m., I got up for school.

Later, I threw up in the bushes next to the bus stop.

"I DON'T BELIEVE YOU"

About a year after Dad's overdose, I ran away from home. I was fourteen. Well, maybe "ran away from home" sounds dramatic. I didn't wrap my meager things in a handkerchief, tie the bundle to the end of a stick, and go walking off into the woods, like Tom Sawyer or anything. And I certainly didn't make a wooden raft, or live on a river island for a few days, or fake my own death, although those things would have been cool—and good for the story line in this book.

What I did do was call Dad and tell him I wanted to live with him. Not because I wanted to live with him. I didn't. But I knew I couldn't live with my mother anymore. I was a teen, and I assumed kids had two options: Mom or Dad. I honestly thought he was my only other option. After that trip to the hospital, we started talking again. Not often, but occasionally—enough for me to know that he was living outside Spanish Fork, Utah, in a small farming community called Lake Shore, in a trailer on his new girlfriend's farm. They had intentions of getting married, or at least that's what he said. Not that I could keep track of his life or relationships at this point. By my count, the woman he was planning to marry would be his fourth wife.

I think.

Or maybe she was his fifth.

As I've said before, I wasn't always invited to the weddings.

It just seemed like every once in a while, he'd introduce me to someone and act like we were best buddies for a moment. Like we had this amazing relationship, which seemed incredibly false to me. He would use the word *buddy* over and over during these introductions, drawing out the *u* in the word with his rural Utah twang. "This here's my buuuuddy. He's my son, you know. But he's also my best buuuuddy."

He'd punch me in the arm and smile, and as much as I hated feeling like a prop in his dating life, I kind of looked forward to these moments. It was like we were actors playing parts—sure, I knew that. But I liked pretending, even for a short time, that we had a good relationship. I liked the way it made me feel, almost like I *did* have an involved, loving father who was interested in me because I was his son and not just because he wanted to look good in front of his new girlfriend.

I wanted to be his buddy.

So I played along for the most part. I smiled, and nodded, and blushed a little when he slugged me gently in the arm, the whole time thinking maybe he was enjoying it, too, and this interaction might lead to his reverting back to that father he used to be before he left my mother.

But what really bugged me each time was when this new woman would be all smiles, and smell like perfume, and ask me to call her Mom.

Dad would wink at me and give me this face that seemed to say, "I need this."

And every single time, I'd say in a flat, matter-of-fact teenager way, "No, lady. There's no freaking way I'm calling you Mom."

Only I didn't say *freaking*.

And—*poof!*—the show was over, the director said cut, and it became awkward in the room as my dad said, "Come on, now. That was uncalled for."

And that was the point in our production where he stopped calling me his buddy.

We did a number of these shows for different women for a year or so, and then he met this woman with the farm, and now he was living on her property, in a trailer.

I knew he was trying to impress her, and so I knew that if I asked to move in with him, he'd probably agree. Part of me hoped that moving in with him would rebuild our relationship. Perhaps it would end up like a sitcom, like *The Fresh Prince of Bel-Air* or something, where I'd move in and it would be awkward at first, but eventually we'd learn to love each other again.

Dad came to his old house, the one with the shop in the backyard. I'd packed my things in garbage sacks, because that's all I could find. I loaded them in the bed of his Ford pickup, the same truck he was driving the night he left my mother. He cranked it over, popped it into gear, and the motor strained as he backed out of the driveway, all of it sounding exactly like it did the night he left almost five years earlier. And as we pulled away, it almost felt like we were reenacting that night all over again, only this time, *I* was walking out on my mother.

Dad and I hardly said a word as he drove.

Mom was working late, cleaning houses. I didn't tell her I was leaving, not because I didn't want her to know, but because I couldn't face her. If I can remember one emotion stemming from my mother's presence, it was fear. I was completely terrified of her. Yes, there were good moments between us from time to time. But on the whole, I found her unpredictable, and angry, and unavailable.

But looking back on this moment—my leaving in the evening with my father, a man who had paid little to no child support, cheated, and time and time again failed to take care of his own children—I cannot help but feel like leaving was the worst thing I'd ever done. I was, without a doubt, turning my back on her, but I was too young to fully understand what that would mean. I was too young to understand how she had to work two, sometimes three, jobs to make ends meet and how deeply weary that can make someone. I was too young to know what it feels like when someone you love, someone you have had children with, someone who you've dedicated your life to chooses someone else when you aren't looking, only to then have your own child leave with that person while you are closing out a fourteen-hour day. I cannot help but think of my mother at this time in our lives and see dedication, hard work, and sacrifice.

But I also know that she was a broken woman. She gave her all to make ends meet, and she had little left emotionally to give her children, and I don't think any of that was her fault. It was just the situation. But all of that came out in these raw moments when she screamed so hard and so fast that the spit from her mouth would sting my face.

And listen, I wasn't a great kid. I wasn't a terrible kid, necessarily. I was more of a mischievous fourteen-year-old boy with a big mouth and a lot of personality. The kind of kid who made too many jokes in class to get attention. I was that kid who got asked pretty regularly to sit in the hallway. I skipped school from time to time to hang out at the local grocery stores or walk to a pizza place, which seemed pretty hard-core and rebellious at the time, but in reality was just stupid. I was horrible about doing homework, which is on-brand for a lot of fourteen-year-olds. I'm raising one right now, and getting him to do his homework is basically a full-time job.

But unlike my friends, I didn't have anyone at home to hassle me about assignments or answer the phone when the school called to talk about some of my classroom antics. I was living in a pretty buttoned-down Mormon community, and compared to my peers, I was probably seen as the devil's assistant because I sometimes used the f-word—but in reality, I was just a troubled kid with a complicated family. My older brother had an after-school job at a call center, the same place where my older sister used to work. And my sister got married that year. No one was home to ask me about assignments, so I just didn't do them.

I was a latchkey kid. I came home from school each day and watched family comedies like *Home Improvement* or *Full House* and longed to have scripted family moments, complete with antics and love and resolution, and I dreaded the moment Mom came home. I found a lot of comfort in those shows.

More than I'd like to admit.

But what I realized at a pretty young age is that when you are even a little rebellious and aloof and not all that interested in anything outside of watching TV and eating gummy bears, and your mother is alone and working ungodly hours to support the family, all of the traits I listed earlier can be like tossing water on a grease fire.

She'd get home late, angry at her situation, and rightly so. But what it looked like to me, as a freshman in high school, was that even when I did my homework, did my chores, had a good day at school, she still yelled at me. She was just mad at the world, and I happened to be the one she came home to.

She called me stupid, lazy, worthless. It caused her to say she wished she'd never had me, that I was a mistake and a burden. Sometimes when she came home, I would hide in my closet and pretend

I was out, hopeful that I would not have to interact with her, because I didn't know what to expect.

I was just so afraid.

I thought about suicide regularly, but I couldn't tell her about that. I didn't want to add more to her already very full plate, so I just started quietly planning it out, going through the motions in my head. The details started to become more and more real, and the week before I left home, I realized that I had two exits from all the fear I was feeling: I could call my dad and try living somewhere else, or I could kill myself.

So I called my dad.

I'm not sure how long I stayed with him, in that small trailer parked on gravel next to a hayfield, but it wasn't very long. Definitely not a week. Probably a few days. I remember thinking that maybe I could make this work. Maybe I could stay with my dad, in this little space, just the two of us, father and son.

Each morning he crawled out of bed in nothing but a pair of tighty-whities. His body was frail, ribs clearly visible, sweat dripping from his hair, hands and legs shaking, eyes bloodshot, skin pale. Then he'd take a handful of pain pills and sit with his arms folded, his head on the table, waiting for his "medicine to start working."

And I remember sitting across from him each morning, wondering if this was normal. Wondering if other kids' parents woke up with the shakes like that. After about twenty minutes with his head down, he'd stand, get dressed, eat, and drive me to school in Provo.

And although I didn't fully understand what was going on with my dad, as I watched him wake up each morning shaking like a naked man in a snowstorm, sweat running down his chest at the same time, I couldn't help but feel anxious about it. It was during these moments that I began to wonder if he was dying. I wondered if he had some long-term ailment, some form of cancer—something—that was killing him and he just wasn't telling anyone. And the thought of losing my father, even when we'd had a checkered relationship, felt very terrifying. Each morning, I ended up taking a trip to the restroom because of those anxious feelings.

During those few days living with Dad, the police called twice. Once to confirm that I'd not been kidnapped. And again to discuss that Mom was planning to charge me with theft for taking my things. And as much as I took pride in the thought of my mother's getting the city to make my dad move his shop, this all felt like I was now on Dad's end of her playbook. At first she was going to press charges but later decided against it.

Trent called once to tell me that Mom was really pissed off and that I needed to come home. I could tell that Mom put him up to this because he was speaking in an authoritative tone that he used only when lying.

"You should leave too," I said.

"No. No. I can't," he said.

His tone changed when he answered me. He

was telling the truth with that last line. He didn't like living with Mom either, but he also felt an obligation to her. I felt that obligation too. But I was so tired of being afraid and feeling uncertain. I still loved her. She was my mother.

But I also knew that when she was around, I felt this tightness in my stomach. It was an intense feeling that would push me to my emotional limit, and when it got bad enough, I'd throw up. Her presence kept me awake, and when she was around, I felt the need to run and hide. The thought of moving back into her home felt like pain inside my stomach. There was a raw fear in me that was taking physical forms: stomach pains, cold sweats, sleepless nights, and moments of uncontrollable shaking. Those physical manifestations, along with thoughts of suicide, overshadowed my sense of duty to my mother. But what I didn't realize as I spoke with my brother was that as I was leaving my mother's home, I was also leaving him. Our relationship was never the same after my departure. Sure, we saw each other. Yes, we spoke on the phone. But slowly, over the years, we just drifted apart, and when I look back, I can see that this phone call was the beginning of our separation.

To my recollection, Mom called me once, after the police and after Trent. I can remember her yelling most of the conversation, telling me I had to come home. She demanded it, actually.

Then she said all the things I was feeling. She said I was abandoning her. She asked, "How can you do this to me?" She called me ungrateful. I just sat in that trailer and listened, and once she'd said everything she needed to, I told her that I loved her. I meant it, but I also said I couldn't come home. However, I never told her why. And when I think back on this moment, I assume I didn't tell her because I was trying to spare her feelings. But I realize that I was only sparing myself. The simple silence I gave her over the phone was a lot like the silence my father gave me the night he walked out after I passed him my poem.

I just wanted this to be over.

Once she'd finished yelling over the phone, there was a long moment of silence, and without either of us saying goodbye, we ended the phone call.

During my last day staying with Dad, he drove me twenty miles north to Provo High. It was dark as we traveled along county roads.

Somewhere between Lake Shore and I-15, Dad said, "Sometimes, when I look at people, I know what they're thinking."

We were both quiet for a moment.

I could see his eyes in the green dashboard lights. They kept glancing at me, and then at the road. I didn't know what to say, so I didn't say anything. He went on.

"When I look at people, I just know. It's like a . . ." He paused for a moment, his calloused right hand tapping the stick shift. "Like I have a signal into their brain. I know exactly what's going on in their heads. I know it sounds crazy to say you can read people's minds, but it's true. I was just wondering if you have it too."

"I don't." I didn't miss a beat with my response.

He stuck out his lower lip and nodded, his motions reminding me of when he found out Grandpa had died four years earlier. It was the face he made while receiving bad news.

"I just wanted you to have it too," he said. "That's all. I'm sorry you don't."

I looked at him in the dark as he drove and thought, *What in the world is wrong with my dad?* I mean, I guess maybe it was possible, but if he could read minds, why was he so bad at human interaction? Why did every romantic relationship he entered go belly-up so spectacularly, and why could he never read how badly I wanted him to just be an active, dependable father, same as he was before he left my mother?

How could he not see that? Any normal human, without telepathy or any other superhuman power, could have seen that. And yet he was completely blind to it.

I didn't tell him he was full of it. I didn't look him in the eyes and ask, "Okay, Brain Wave, what am I thinking?" And I didn't point to someone on the street and demand, "What's going on in that head, smart guy?" Not that it would have proven anything. I was not aware of any way to confirm what he was saying outside of asking him to read my mind—and if he did offer to read my thoughts, it wouldn't be difficult. At that moment, everything I was thinking was written flatly on my face: *My dad's an empty saltshaker.*

He dropped me off at school, and as I walked

into the main building, all I could do was gaze at other students. I looked at their faces and hands, shoulders and strides, and I couldn't believe how quickly I went from thinking Dad was nuts to wondering if maybe I had this power too. I'd long assumed there was something wrong with my dad, but I'd never suspected he was completely crazy. I knew it was impossible to read minds, and yet I wanted it to be true because then Dad would be exceptional instead of mad. All of it would turn into one of those comic book origin stories, and when Dad saved the world during an alien invasion with his telepathy, I wouldn't have to be so ashamed of him anymore.

I attended gym class that morning, and I blatantly stared at this kid in the locker room for an exceptionally long period of time—trying to grab anything from his mind, trying to see if I had my father's mind-reading power—until this boy I didn't know looked me up and down and said, "If you look at me one more time, I'm going to punch you in the balls."

And to be honest, I didn't see that coming.

Not at all.

So I looked at the ground out of fear, sure, but it was also a reflective moment. It was then that I decided I couldn't live with Dad either.

I don't remember the day I moved in with my grandmother. I don't remember trying to explain my reasoning to her. I don't remember putting my shirts in the closet or packing my baggy jeans in the dresser.

Chances are I took the school bus to her house and just never left. Dad probably brought my things at some point.

What I do remember very clearly, though, were the first several days after I moved in. Once it was established that I wouldn't be leaving, I sat on Grandma's plaid sofa next to the woodburning fireplace in her living room paneled with faux wood, which gave the room the feel of a log cabin, and felt this wave of comfort. I finally felt safe. I felt safer than I'd ever felt, and it was easily the warmest, most pleasant emotion I'd ever experienced. And I remember there were conditions for me to live there: I would attend church and I would keep my hair short, two rules I went on to break.

If I walked to the back of Grandma's farm and looked over the grass and cows, I could see my mom's house in the distance, but after I left her home, Mom and I spoke only intermittently. Sometimes I visited on holidays. We also spent two short vacations together, one to Las Vegas and another to Jackson Hole, Wyoming. But on the whole, we often went months without speaking to or seeing each other, and this silence lasted for seven years.

Grandma's home was the stablest place I'd ever been. Each morning she got up at six o'clock, listened to local news on KSL-AM, and made toast, a hot cup of Pero (a coffee substitute), and Wheat Hearts with milk and butter. On Tuesdays she went to Ream's grocery store and Sundays she went to church. She wore sweatpants and scuffed white sneakers, and in the winter she wore a faded yellow coat. When she hugged me, which was at least twice a day, her arms trembled, and so did her lips when she kissed my cheek. Her home had the same floral-print carpet and brown and white tile it did in '82, the year I was born. She was dependable, unwavering, the rock of my young life. Moving in with Grandma granted me the emotional support my mother simply didn't have to give and the calm, sane consistency my father was unable to provide.

And I think my living with Grandma gave her something to live for too. Or at least that's what I told myself. She was in her late seventies. I'm not sure how long my grandfather had been dead. Probably three or four years by the time I moved in, and during that time, she lived alone, caring for her home and yard. She didn't do much farmwork anymore; my uncle handled most of that.

Grandpa's awards for land management still hung next to the kitchen door. The silver toaster he bought in the '70s still sat next to the refrigerator. The farm equipment and the land he tilled with it surrounded Grandma's redbrick home. I would sometimes catch Grandma sitting in her white vinyl rocking chair, looking out the patio windows, same as she did when Grandpa worked the alfalfa field—her expression, the softness of her eyes, it was all the same, almost like she could still see him.

She gave me the room my aunts used to share. Or maybe it's because it was the room I chose.

It was pretty girly, I'll admit, with the yellow print bedspread and matching curtains. However, it was also the only bedroom in the house with a TV and VCR—and those were things I simply couldn't pass up.

The whole house smelled musty, like when sheets are left in the closet too long. The majority of the food in the cupboards was stale, particularly the breakfast cereal, and all of it was old-people food, with *Bran* or *Oats* in every brand name.

She didn't have cable or a dishwasher, and she still had a rotary phone. But none of that seemed to matter, because she was always there when I needed her.

Always.

But even with the change of scenery, my anxiety continued to develop. Shortly after I moved in, my dad started running into trouble with the law. I remember hearing he'd gotten arrested, and I started to experience chronic anxiety-related diarrhea as a result. It was a pretty nasty problem that came on suddenly and dramatically and lasted into my early twenties.

At the time, I didn't know what my father had done exactly. No one would tell me. I'd just overhear things as Grandma spoke on the phone to my aunt. I heard he'd been charged with a crime, but I wasn't sure if he went to jail. I know that Grandma gave him some money to get a lawyer and some more money to pay something called *restitution*, a word I was unfamiliar with at the time.

Eventually, I pieced together that he'd been

caught passing bad checks to everyone from auto parts stores, to gas stations, to pharmacies. It's funny—when I was in my late teens, I went to a pharmacy close to my house, and on the wall next to the register was a list of people the pharmacy would not accept checks from. Naturally, my dad's name was listed. Looking back now, I realize he was probably passing bad checks to pay for pain meds. At the time, I didn't realize someone could get charged with a misdemeanor for that sort of thing. In fact, I didn't know the difference between a misdemeanor and a felony, which was probably a good thing.

The moment your father begins to become an outlaw, even a petty one, it's difficult not to look at yourself and not feel anxious as you wonder if you're destined for the same misguided future. And it's also hard for the mother of that same man not to look at her grandson, who is living in her home, and wonder the same thing.

I suppose it's time to admit that at about the same time, after several months of my living with Grandma, the honeymoon phase was over.

Not that she ever yelled at me like my mother. And she never drifted in and out of my life like my father. Rather, what I got from my grandmother was a frank consistency. One hundred percent no bull. She had expectations for homework. She had a curfew, and she was pretty critical of my friends, referring to many of them as "crum-bums" and "jackwagons."

"You need to stop hanging out with so many

crum-bums," she'd say. "Those kids look like a bunch of go-nowhere jackwagons! Is that what you wanna be? A jackwagon?"

To this day, I'm not 100 percent sure what a jackwagon is. But I pieced together that it wasn't something she wanted me to become. Yet, in her estimation, I was heading in that direction very quickly, with my refusal to get a haircut, and my bad grades, and my pant legs that were so baggy and long that every time it rained they drew in gallons of water, until the soaked denim drifted so far up my leg it actually reached my butt cheeks.

She had a lot of opinions about my clothing, particularly my pants. The first time she saw me in a pair of JNCO jeans, a brand that was popular in the '90s for reasons I still can't explain, she appeared almost dizzy. It was a dazed look, the kind of confused expression someone might make after hitting their head during a car accident. The jeans' leg openings were nearly the same circumference as the waist. We were in the kitchen. She sat in her white rocker, looking me up and down, clearly fazed by how awesome I looked. Or so I suspected. I was asking her a question, but she interrupted by reaching out and tugging on one of my pant legs near the thigh. "So you're wearing maternity pants now?" she asked.

I had no idea what maternity pants were, so I just said, "Yeah, I guess."

Grandma put her hand over her face and let out a long sigh that seemed to say, "I'm raising an idiot."

I was not allowed to date until I was sixteen.

This was according to Mormon standards, so by the time I was fifteen, when girls started to call, even if it was for a church event, or a group homework assignment, she'd pick up the phone, make an assessment of their voice, and, if it sounded too feminine, she would flatly say, "Girls shouldn't call boys." Then she'd slam her rotary phone down hard enough to sting their ears, and let out a "humph" like she'd just taught some youngster a very good lesson on boy-girl interactions. These moments were particularly awkward for me as a young boy interested in girls, sure, but they were especially difficult for those male friends of mine that were a little late in the puberty game and still sounded a lot like their sister.

She hassled me about the music I listened to and the movies and TV shows I watched. She told me I needed to eat meat and potatoes with every meal, because it would help me grow strong, and she had a pretty casual relationship with bacon, insisting that it was part of a healthy diet. Sometimes she made me sandwiches that were nothing more than toasted and buttered bread with a dozen strips of bacon. I loved those bacon sandwiches, but as I write this sentence as a thirty-eight-year-old man, I cannot help but wonder what long-term damage they had on my arteries, and I have a feeling I'm still working that crap through my colon.

I know those of you reading this have questions as to how my grandmother lived so long eating red meat 24-7, and all I can say is that she seemed to have been made of something different than other people, something stronger, something that could tear through a steak the size of a toilet seat without remorse or even heartburn.

I remember her insisting that I learn to play an instrument, so I chose the guitar because I assumed it would impress girls—a fact that never, not even a little bit, worked out for me. Probably because I wasn't very good, and I didn't practice as much as I should have, and I couldn't for the life of me keep time. When I did play in front of a girl, it was mostly me hitting a few power chords, with long pauses in which I said, "Just a minute. I can do this. Just a minute."

Eventually she would yawn, and well . . . None of this was attractive.

Ironically, though, before Grandma agreed to buy me a guitar, she tried very hard to persuade me to learn the accordion. She was a huge fan of *The Lawrence Welk Show*, a musical variety program that she watched almost religiously on PBS. It had comedy I didn't get because all the jokes were dated, but Grandma nearly fell out of her chair laughing with each episode.

She had stacks of records, and I can still remember her watching that show and insisting that I sit and join her as she clapped, and sang along, and then looked at me, hopeful that I'd find it as inspirational as she did. There were accordions, and sparkly cowboy costumes, and frankly it was the nerdiest thing I'd ever seen. Just watching it made me feel less attractive, and I was already short for my age and covered with white-headed pimples, with a cracking voice and emotional problems, so the thought of watching a show that made me feel less attractive was almost too much. But as a dutiful grandson, I humored her, and at least once a week we sat together and watched *The Lawrence Welk Show*.

I remember Grandma pulling an old accordion out of the hall closet and showing it to me with glee, saying, "I'd be honored if you'd learn to play this like your father." I had no idea that he used to play the accordion. Apparently when he lost the fingers from his left hand, he couldn't play anymore. However, it quickly became a side of him I tried not to imagine, but I was forced to after she insisted that I try it. I stood in the living room with this albatross of an instrument hanging from my chest, feeling like it was more or less a chastity belt. Grandma gazed at me, her eyes almost tearful, her hand over her mouth, as though I were actually Lawrence Welk himself. My face was red, body awkward, all of it very similar to Ralphie from *A Christmas Story* in his pink bunny pajamas.

Ultimately, I declined to play the accordion for a number of reasons—mostly because I wanted to meet girls, and playing the accordion felt like a surefire way to never, ever have a romantic relationship with anyone. But more importantly, I was trying very hard not to be my father, and playing his old instrument didn't jibe with that, so after weeks of back-and-forth, Grandma finally agreed to buy me an acoustic guitar (even though I'd asked for an electric). But I was happy to get it considering the alternative was to play an instrument that was, in my teenage opinion, the same as being forced into a life of celibacy.

She helped me find a guitar teacher in downtown Provo whom I met with once a week. One time Grandma was driving home from a lesson, and this man stepped out in front of her car. He wasn't anywhere near a crosswalk. He was just walking in the street. And I'll just say it: He was an intimidating-looking dude, with long grizzled hair and a beard. He wore black leather boots with a faded and stained black Ozzy Osbourne *Diary of a Madman* T-shirt and tight jeans with holes in the knees. His whole look was letting the world know that the '80s were very good to him. He was holding a brown paper bag of what I assumed was booze. He smacked the hood of Grandma's car with his palm, and yelled, "I'm walking!" Then he called her something along the lines of an old b, and wow. That got her fired up. All of it felt like we were in New York City rather than downtown Provo, Utah.

She slammed the gray Buick my grandfather bought her shortly before he died into park and honked the horn in those long, angry honks that mean you're ready to punch someone in the face. He started cursing at her some more, and I don't know if it was the red meat, or living through the Depression, or having spent so many hours in the hot Utah sun doing farmwork, or just general frustration about having to raise a teenager at her age, but I kid you not, Grandma unrolled the driver's side window, practically stuck all five-foot-two of herself—old-lady perm and all—out of it, and yelled, "You need to watch your language, son!" Her right finger was wagging. He looked at her with this slack-jawed, terrified look, almost like she wasn't simply some old lady in a gray Buick but his own honest-to-goodness mother.

"And you need to get out of the street, because next time someone is going to run your stupid kiester over!" She looked him up and down, and when he didn't move, she started to casually shoo him toward the sidewalk with a wave of her hand, like she might address a stubborn house cat. And this guy, this tough dude that I, as a fifteen-year-old kid, would have never tangled with, just went along with it. Once he made it to the sidewalk, she sat back in her seat, rolled up the window, put the car in gear, and slammed on the gas, peeling out a little.

I was in awe.

It was moments like this that I realized my grandmother wasn't someone to trifle with. So like any reasonable fifteen-year-old child would do, I lied. I lied about everything, and I think part of the problem was that I often lied to myself.

I told myself the diarrhea I was experiencing was irritable bowel syndrome, something I'd heard about in a biology class. IBS felt like an unfortunate and embarrassing ailment, sure, but it was biological, and it seemed less embarrassing than admitting that those anxious feelings I was battling three or four times a week were causing my bowels to flood. Admitting it was anxiety felt like admitting I was crazy, and that seemed too close to my father's example.

I was also grappling with the reality that even when your situation changes, even when things get better and you find safety from a chaotic place and time, your anxiety can still linger. In many ways my life was better. I had someone in my life I could depend on in the ways I needed as a young boy. Yet my anxiety, that fear I felt before moving in with Grandma, was still there, and that was a tough pill for me to swallow. But keeping with that code of silence I learned from my mother, I didn't mention any of this to anyone, not even my grandmother.

I didn't want to be like my dad or my mom. I was old enough to see that, and yet I couldn't help but mimic the way they managed things. Like my mother, I denied my anxiety to myself and to others. That self-denial led to a nasty habit of dishonesty, a skill I acquired from my father. I lied all the time to cover for my anxiety. I lied to hide that I lived with my grandmother and not my parents, telling people outlandish stories about how my mom was in Hollywood trying to make it as an actress and my dad was a bull-riding cowboy competing in the PBR.

I remember telling friends, teachers, anyone who would listen, "Once a year, we all get together as a family. They tell me about their amazing lives. Dad gives me a few of the buckles he's won, and Mom gives me some things she picked up around

LA. It's always wonderful."

No one believed me, but it was easier to live with people thinking I was full of it than to admit that my mom and I hardly spoke and my dad was starting to have trouble with the law. I lied because the truth was far too difficult, and it was the truth that sat deep in my gut and came flooding out my anus.

I suppose what I am most ashamed of is that I lied to Grandma more than anyone else. I spent hours in the restroom, crouching, grunting, and sweating. I turned on the tub to hide the sound. When Grandma knocked and asked what I was doing, I told her I was taking a bath.

"Why do you take so many baths?" she once asked.

"I don't know," I said. "I just like being clean."

I'm not sure what she assumed I was up to, but I think she knew I wasn't always taking a bath, and I was going through puberty, so I'm sure she did the math and realized it was something she didn't want to address head-on.

Lying about my diarrhea led to compulsive, bizarre lies. I told her the school gave me a scholarship to attend Space Camp, when really I just wanted to spend the weekend with a friend. I wrecked my bike and came home with a black eye and scuffed knees. I told her a cougar attacked me next to the Provo River. I was full of crap, a truth confirmed regularly as I sat grunting on the toilet.

My lies, my anxious diarrhea, all of it came to a head during freshman PE. The class was playing softball on a far-off stretch of grass. We must have been at least half a mile away from the main campus. I caught a ball and it knocked something loose. My stomach turned, and instantly I needed a restroom.

Bad.

Real bad.

I dropped the ball and ran—but I couldn't run the whole way, only in short bursts, slowing every dozen strides to flex my cheeks. I can only imagine what people thought of me as I sprinted from the field and across campus. I probably looked like a street-corner madman, running in these crazed zombie-like sprints and then stopping suddenly to flex my lower body, contort my hips, and grab my butt cheeks, moving in whatever ways were necessary to keep going forward while also keeping whatever was trying to get out from actually getting out.

Once next to the main buildings, I had two options. One restroom was in the new wing. This restroom was clean and boasted a lilac-scented air freshener. The other restroom was in the old wing, across from the metal and wood shops. It smelled of grease, wood shavings, and urine. Several of the toilet seats were missing.

Naturally, the old wing was the closest.

I was just outside the wood shop when I had to grab my butt and pinch my cheeks together.

It worked! I was going to make it. But just before I reached the restroom doors, my stomach calmed. I felt fine, and I suppose I got greedy.

I really didn't want to use the old wing's restroom—I
don't think anyone in my high school ever did—so
I made a dangerous play. I headed for the cleaner
restrooms.

Two steps later, it happened.

I lost it in my gym shorts, and I found it in my
socks.

I went back to the nasty old-wing restroom and,
as I examined the damage and then took in the
smell of it all, I felt this wave of terror. I realized
that I was very alone, in high school, with poop
all over the back of my pants, and down my socks,
and even in the back of my shoes, and I had no
idea what to do or how to get help, so I looked at
myself in the cracked mirror and tried not to cry—
but ultimately cried a little. I took a deep breath,
blew my nose, and then cleaned myself with toilet
paper as best I could.

I quickly realized that from the front I looked
normal, and I devised a plan that wasn't exactly
brilliant, but it was simple and cunning, and I
thought that it just might save me from being known
as Poop Kid or Poopy Pants Edwards or simply The
Turd for the rest of my high school career.

I left the restroom and kept my back to the
hall wall, moving in this awkward side shuffle so
no one would see the back of my shorts. I was
heading to the closest pay phone, with plans to
call my grandmother.

I was getting close to making it out of the
school when I ran into an open classroom door,
something I hadn't calculated for. If I crossed, all

the people in the room would've seen my poopy pants. I imagined it playing out. One kid would notice first and scream, "Hey, that kid crapped his pants!" And then the laughter would come with damning statements mingled in: "He smells like a nursing home," "He'll never get a girlfriend now," and the worst coming from the attractive brunette in the front row, "And I used to like you."

I quickly crossed the hall. I was forced to do this three more times before making it to the pay phone.

No one saw me, for which I was grateful.

Once outside, I called Grandma collect.

"I need you to pick me up," I said. "Right now?"

She asked why, and I told her a nonsense story about a bomb at the high school. "It's being evacuated," I said.

To be fair, I shouldn't have lied. But honestly, who wants to tell anyone, particularly their grandmother, that they crapped their pants at school? And sure, she probably was going to figure out what had happened the moment she picked me up, but I really was taking this moment by moment, and I assumed I'd figure out the rest when the time came.

She paused, exhaled, and exclaimed, "Bologna! Are you in trouble?"

I didn't respond.

"Dang it, Clint," she said. "You're just like your father. Whenever he gets in trouble, he calls me collect and tells some cock-and-bull story and I come running. I'm done with this business." She paused for a moment, clearly waiting for me to come clean, give her the truth. But when I didn't, she filled the silence. "Is that what you want? To end up in trouble like your father? 'Cause that's where you're headed."

She was fed up, and I was hit with two different emotions. One of them was fear that she was officially done with my antics and would be kicking me out at any moment. But that fear was overshadowed pretty quickly as I was overcome with the reality of her comparison to my father. I was already terrified that I would eventually become him. That notion was becoming more and more real in my mind each day, so to have someone who knew me as well as Grandma compare me to him so flatly, well, it caused my legs to tremble and made me think, for a moment, that I was going to need another trip to the restroom.

"I crapped my pants," I said with sincerity, honesty, and fear.

It was quiet again for a moment. I could hear the click of Grandma rearranging her dentures with her tongue, something she often did when mulling something over. Eventually she said, "I don't believe you. You're a grown boy."

We went back and forth, Grandma attempting to uncover the truth and I repeating it in a forceful whisper, hopeful that it would sink in.

Eventually I said, "Please, please, please come. And bring a towel." Perhaps it was the terror in my voice, or maybe it was that I asked for a towel, but she agreed.

I sat outside, my back against a brick wall, and

waited. I smelled terrible. Time passed. I told a math instructor I broke my leg and I was waiting for a ride. I told the secretary that my house was on fire and I was waiting for a firefighter. And I told the truancy officer that my brother had had an accident on a roller coaster. "A bolt came loose and busted him in the head," I said. He wished me luck.

I don't think any of them believed me, but they didn't question me further, and I was comfortable with that.

I was scanning the road for Grandma when I saw Samantha Jones. I was completely in love with her. She was the only girl I knew who enjoyed Metallica. Her glasses were thick, with heavy brown frames that matched her hair. She was just the right mix of nerd and rebel. She wasn't taller than I was, which was a big deal considering I might have been five foot four by this point—but maybe not. At night, my imagination projected flickering films of Samantha onto the ceiling: Samantha gracefully ascending stairs, her hair blowing in the wind.

I tried not to make eye contact with her, hoping that she wouldn't notice me, but it didn't work. She was a hugger. She hugged everyone she knew, and maybe people she only sorta knew, and we knew each other pretty well, so the moment she saw me, she cried out my name and sprinted toward me. And like an idiot, I stood so she could hug me. A hug from Samantha Jones was every-thing. I wanted to smell what I, as a teenager, believed was absolutely charming perfume, but was most likely just her melon-scented deodorant.

But all I could smell was my own crap.

We separated and exchanged a glance.

She knew.

Her nose scrunched and she swatted it.

"What smells?" she said.

"I don't smell anything."

She leaned in and took a sniff. I waved my hand in front of her nose in a vain attempt to circulate the air.

"You smell terrible. Did you crap yourself or something?"

"No!"

I was a mix of anxiety, cold sweat, love, and lust. She smiled, half laughed, and then grabbed my left shoulder and attempted to turn me around.

"Let me see your butt."

She peeked over one shoulder and then the other as I moved my hips from side to side, and for a moment it felt like we were dancing, which was something I'd have loved to do with Samantha Jones. But not like this.

Never like this.

She asked what was on my socks, and I told her that's just how they looked. We went back and forth for a moment more, and finally she said, "If you didn't crap yourself, then what smells like a turd?"

"I don't know," I said. "Probably you?"

It was a pathetic, childish refute. Samantha's narrowed eyes and rigid shoulders, the way her jaw moved from side to side seemed to say, "You *did* crap yourself!"

And as she walked away, I knew she was never going to speak to me again.

Grandma honked the horn. She was in a gray sweatshirt, the sleeves pushed up to the elbows, her hair neatly permed.

She leaned across the seat, opened the passenger door, and said, "Get in."

I placed the towel across the seat and sat down. As we drove, Grandma rolled down all the windows in her Buick and told me I smelled rotten.

We drove in silence for a while, a cool midmorning wind jetting across our faces. Part of me was still worried that she was going to call our time together, my living with her—all of it—quits and send me to live with one of my parents. I assumed that all the lies, and now this nasty, immature moment, was just too much for her. Part of me wanted to ask if she was done with me, but I was afraid, so I just sat there silently, looking at the road.

"I'm sorry I didn't believe you," she said.

Then she let out a breath and told me of a time when Dad was fourteen. He had called home, just like I had, and told her some ridiculous story that she couldn't recall. He'd said he needed a ride home. When she picked him up, he had a black eye.

"He'd been in a fight," she said, "and he didn't want anyone to know he'd lost. I didn't want anyone to know he'd been in a fight. So I took him home and put makeup on his eye. I did it each morning until it healed."

She didn't say anything for a while. Once our

house was within view she said, "I've been covering up his mistakes for some time. Trying to believe his lies. Maybe that's why he's such a mess."

This was the first time Grandma had ever spoken to me so frankly about my father.

We were parked in the garage of Grandma's home, the garage door still open. She looked me in the eyes. "People are smarter than you think," she said. "Telling lies will catch up with you."

And for the first time, I confided in her. I told her the truth. I told her about the stomach pains and the way my hands would shake. I told her I was scared all the time and that when the fear became too much, I got diarrhea, and that's what had happened today. "But I'm scared to tell anyone about it, because I think it means I'm crazy."

I was more honest with her than I'd ever been with anyone else about what was going on in my body and my mind. I was probably more honest with her than I'd ever been with myself.

She sat and quietly listened.

Then she did something I didn't expect.

Something I didn't see coming at all.

She admitted to me that the same things happened to her when she got nervous. She referred to them jokingly as her "poop-haps."

We both laughed at that, and then she told me that she often got those tight feelings in her stomach too. "I don't think it means you're crazy, sweetheart. Unless that means I'm crazy. Do you think Grandma is crazy?"

I shook my head, and I asked when she started

getting them.

She thought, and said, "I started getting them when I was your age, I think. But times were hard then." I knew she was talking about the Depression. She mentioned that a lot. "They've been with me for so long it's hard to remember exactly when they started." She was quiet for a moment. Then she said, "I've been having a lot of those feelings recently because of your father." She thought for a moment, and I wondered if I was causing her some of those feelings as well.

She patted my knee, and apologized again for not believing me when I called. And as uncomfortable as it was to chat with a woman in her seventies about our shared poop-haps and anxiety, my pants full of diarrhea, the windows of her gray Buick rolled all the way down, we truly bonded that day. But more than anything, she made me feel less alone. This was the first time anyone close to me had admitted that they suffered from anxiety. I didn't realize it at the moment, but looking back, I know that what I needed more than anything was to find someone else who shared my same ailment. I don't know if I'd ever felt so grateful for my grandmother.

"Go take a bath, sweetheart," Grandma said. "I'll wash your clothes."

BAD ASS COFFEE

My older brother, Trent, was eighteen and in college, which was kind of new and strange considering no one in our family had ever left home for college. In the years before Trent left for college, he and I had drifted apart. He'd moved to Pleasant Grove, about twenty minutes away from Grandma's house, when my mother remarried. I knew that he'd earned an Eagle Scout award and spoke of serving on a two-year Mormon mission. He quoted Mormon prophets and apostles in casual conversation and was prone to saying, "I prayed for you last night."

He was attending a state university nearly three hours north of Provo. He didn't have a going-away party. I never saw his gray Reliant filled with moving boxes. I never hugged him warmly before he pulled from the driveway and headed north on I-15. Like he did most things, Trent quietly left. I didn't fully realize he was gone until he called me during his first semester.

He spoke in a nervous whisper.

"Dude, I had sex," he said.

He described the experience so rapidly I had a difficult time making out the full details, but words such as *naked* and *dorm room* and *awesome* were easily discernible. But before I had a chance to ask any questions, he hung up.

Trent visited Grandma and me a few days later. His tone was assertive, and when he entered, he did so with a confident swagger, his heels never hitting the floor, his shoulders swaying. He was a slender teen, close to six foot, and he was wearing a Hawaiian shirt, khaki cargo shorts, and flip-flops as though he'd just returned from some tropical island instead of a nearly desertlike climate north of Salt Lake City. He clearly hadn't gotten a haircut since he left, and his trim, Mormon missionary-style cut that was always parted on the side had gradually grown into some sort of half mullet. He also appeared to be making an honest effort at a mustache-goatee combo

When Trent entered our home, Grandma said, "You are glowing."

She was sitting in the white vinyl rocker next to the refrigerator. Trent leaned down to give her a hug and Grandma held him tightly, her hands gripping his shoulders.

"You even feel smarter," she said.

She asked him questions about his classes and the dorms and if he'd made friends.

"Oh yes," he said. "One friend is very special." He looked at me as I stood next to the kitchen counter and gave me a subtle grin.

Her assumption was that his college classes had changed him. But when Trent smiled at me, I knew it was sex that had given him this new confidence.

Later that day, Trent and I were chatting in my room. On my wall was a poster of Mike Myers dressed as Austin Powers, a movie I considered to be edgy, almost rebellious. Trent looked at it for a while and told me about drinking and smoking while watching *The Godfather*.

"Isn't that movie rated R?" I asked. It was commonly understood that we shouldn't watch R-rated movies.

"Screw the church," Trent said while waving his hand.

I paused for a moment to let his words sink in.

Our conversation went on. Trent talked trash about political leaders and religious organizations. He must have used the f-word more than a dozen times, using it to describe everything from his school, to Bill Clinton, to Provo, Utah. Everything had a problem, and he had many, many opinions, and all of them needed emphasizing. He did, however, hesitate before each f-bomb, almost like the word was a stone in his throat that took some effort to push out. During those breaks in his sentences, I could see a glimpse of the staunchly religious teen he had been only a few months earlier.

But without a doubt, Trent had become the most rebellious person I'd ever met. Don't get me wrong, I knew kids in high school who claimed to have had sex, but I didn't believe them. Trent, though, I believed. I'd never criticized the school system, or the U.S. government, or the Mormon church. I was pretty quick to pray about every-thing. Bad things happened and I prayed. Good things happened and I prayed. I prayed for the Spirit of the Lord to reside in my home, for Dad to clean up his life, for my mother to be safe, for my grandmother's health, and for better grades. I attended church for three hours every Sunday.

I was no rebel, but I had been growing my hair out, and wearing baggy clothing, and listening to punk rock that actively swapped out guitar solos with long, angry stings of swears. And yes, I used the occasional f-bomb. The idea of being a rebel sounded appealing as I looked at my very cool older brother. But as I look back on the scene, Trent sitting on the edge of my bed in that Hawaiian shirt, I realize he looked a lot more like a middle-aged father of three on a cruise ship—it was more his demeanor, his aura, his overall vibe that seemed to be seeping rebellion, regardless of his snappy outfit.

Grandma often said, "Be part of the world but not of it." I always interpreted this idiom to mean socialize, but don't give in to temptation. Whenever she said it, though, I found myself thinking about the world beyond the Mormon church. A world I knew only through TV shows like *Melrose Place* and *Beverly Hills, 90210*. Even Tim Taylor, my idealized TV father, casually drank coffee. I didn't know what to make of things like that. I assumed that outside of Provo everything was casual—sex, alcohol, pot, and coffee. I wondered what it was like to be so casual, and I assumed that life outside Utah and the Mormon church was like the Emerald City—a glowing, energetic place at the end of a yellow brick road where I could become something closer to cool.

And let me get one thing straight. I did not feel cool. There was very little about my lifestyle that seemed cool, and at fifteen years old, feeling cool, looking cool, *being* cool sounded like one notch below being a Greek god.

At least once a week Trent called to tell me stories of drunken college parties and sex in the woods. I'm not sure how much of this was true, but I had to assume that it was at least mostly true—and even if it was only 50 percent true, that was hands down the most debauchery I'd ever been exposed to, so I clung to every single word.

To me, Trent became a seasoned traveler with exciting stories of life outside the Mormon church and Provo, Utah. And as much as I loved living with my grandmother, as much as I valued her home and the calm consistency it granted me, there was something about living on a beef and hay farm in the middle of rural Utah that felt like solitary confinement.

The plains of farmland surrounding my home were isolating. I didn't cherish the dirt or respect its ability to bear life. I'd driven a tractor a couple of times and ridden a horse once. Wandering the fields were cows, moving slowly, bellowing, and whipping their tails. Summer days were spent alone, watching *Maury* and *The Price Is Right* and eating gummy worms. Barbed wire fences bordered the acres of farmland surrounding Grandma's home like the walls of a prison yard, and I often looked at the sea of dirty green pasture and longed to toss a rope to civilization and drag it a little closer. So to have a brother who had ventured off into unknown land—and found sex and drugs and other debauchery I'd only heard about—felt like some amazing messenger was coming to me, bringing gold, herbs, and spices.

So when Trent asked if I wanted to try coffee sometime, I thought about Dad. He was the only other person I knew who had left the Mormon church. I knew that Dad drank coffee, but he hid it from us by drinking it when we weren't around or saying that his thermos was full of hot cocoa when I could smell otherwise. I always thought he didn't want to be a bad example. Now I wonder if it was because he didn't want us to tell Grandma. Whatever his reasons for hiding his coffee, it was clear that he enjoyed it. He often sipped and then exhaled loudly and passionately, and sometimes he mumbled, "That's good."

Trent's offer seemed like an opportunity to be cool, to rebel. But most importantly, it seemed like a way to better understand my dad and his life outside the Mormon church.

The day after Trent's invitation was a Sunday. I made an appointment with my bishop so I could ask him why Mormons don't drink coffee. This was the first time I'd ever asked why about anything religious. When I think back on this moment, I realize how prescriptive the Mormon church was in the '90s. I'd always been told not to drink coffee, but never why not. At the time, I assumed it was the caffeine, but apparently that wasn't the case.

My bishop at the time was an engineer who also owned a horse farm. He looked a lot like Christopher Reeve, with dark hair and a strong jaw, and I often felt like I was talking to Superman when I talked to him. And I know that sounds like I was hero-worshipping or even idolizing my bishop, which really wasn't the case. He just really looked like Superman, and I couldn't stop imagining him in blue tights with red underwear over the top, lounging around in the Fortress of Solitude—and that doesn't sound like idolizing at all, but rather a borderline strange sexual fantasy, which really isn't a good place to be mentally when talking to a Mormon bishop.

He began the conversation by reminding me about the importance of going on a two-year mission. "Nineteen is just around the corner," he said. "It'll be here before you know it."

I asked him about coffee and he said, "We don't really know why the Lord asked us not to drink coffee, but in Joseph Smith's time we also didn't know why the Lord advised us not to smoke tobacco." He paused for a moment, leaned back in his chair, did one of those gesturing-to-everything kind of hand movements, and said, "Now it's clear why he asked us not to. It is just a matter of time before people fully understand the why, but right now, you kind of have to go on faith. But in my opinion, you believe in the church, you need to believe in the doctrine as a whole. If someone is going to leave the church over something as silly as coffee, they probably weren't all that committed anyway."

And I'll admit, that last bit, that last explanation actually made sense to me. But the lure, the draw of being as cool as my older brother was just too much. So I called Trent later that day and agreed to join him for coffee.

We drove the forty-five minutes from Provo to Salt Lake to get to Bad Ass Coffee. We left Grandma's house in the evening. Trent chose Bad Ass Coffee because, as far as he knew, Provo had no coffee shops (which was, as far as I knew, true at the time), and Trent didn't want my first coffee experience to be at some pancake house or gas station.

As we drove, Trent told me about sex, drinking on Sundays, and coffee. Cappuccino, double tall mocha, French roast, hazelnut, and cinnamon. He listed the flavors like someone might list fine wines or exotic cars. "Coffee is amazing," he said. He told me it would change my life, open up a new world, and I thought of sunsets beyond the Wasatch Front. I thought about how Dad sipped coffee in his pickup and then sighed with relief. I thought about all the movie stars that started each day with a cup of joe and wondered if maybe, just maybe, this change would be the first step toward Hollywood stardom.

I sat in the passenger seat and gazed at I-15 through the off-balance headlights of Trent's car. I watched the farmland become suburbs and then watched as the suburbs became businesses. As we got closer to the heart of Salt Lake City, I noticed fewer Mormon churches along the freeway, and it felt like we were getting closer to the world outside Mormonism. Not that this was my first time traveling to the city, but this trip, this adventure felt different than before. My senses became heightened. I was nervous and excited, fearful that we would get caught, but I didn't know by whom.

Trent's right hand sat at noon on the steering wheel. His car didn't have an in-dash CD player, so Trent hooked his Discman into the tape deck with a RadioShack adapter. Jimmy Buffett asked if we liked getting caught in the rain as desert wind rocked the car, and I thought to myself, *No. I don't like getting caught in the rain, but I can change, Jimmy Buffett. I can change.*

We pulled into Salt Lake City and then into the parking lot of Bad Ass Coffee. On the roof was a large plastic donkey wearing a bright yellow sombrero. It must have been close to 9:00 p.m., awfully late to be shopping for coffee, but we didn't know that.

My junior high music teacher, a short, toad-faced, snooty woman with a holier-than-thou disposition, once discussed the evils of coffee with the class. She told us that coffee turns your teeth black, gives you kidney stones, and smells like sin. "The only reason people drink it is to offset the effects of alcohol," she said. I sat in on similar discussions with church leaders and family members, and I'm pretty sure this is why I assumed coffee was a controlled substance. This thought had lingered during the drive, but I never voiced it until we entered the coffee shop's parking lot.

"Will they check our IDs?" I asked.

Trent laughed and said, "Don't worry about that. Just think about how cool this is."

I kind of assumed he'd gotten us fake IDs, and I felt this wave of terror, like I'd gotten in over my head and this trip for coffee was going to end in prison time. That was, until I realized the building was dark.

They were closed.

As I looked at the empty coffee shop, I thought about the life experiences I'd been sheltered from. My Sunday school instructors told me to block out the evils of the outside world, but as we sat outside the coffee shop, I wondered if the world was blocking *me* out. Had word of Mormon travelers spread, so they cooled the French roast and locked the doors, excluding us because of the faith we were born into?

Trent banged his hand against the steering wheel and, after a short pause, began to swear.

We sat alone in the parking lot of the closed coffee shop for some time. We tried to find another coffee shop, but we were running out of time. We needed to head home soon or I was going to get into trouble with Grandma.

In an act of determination, Trent pulled into a Chevron. We walked to the back of the gas station. We poured cups of coffee. Trent told me he'd tried it before—he'd listed flavors and roasts that no coffee novice could know—but I suspected by the way his hand shook, by the way he cracked the Styrofoam cup a little with his grip, that this might also have been his first cup of joe. I wasn't sure about it, but I wondered. And in a way, it made me feel relieved, like we were suddenly fellow travelers now.

We ventured into the world outside Mormonism together. We didn't add sugar or cream because we didn't know about them. I sniffed the black liquid as Trent said, "This is going to be amazing."

We walked to the car, our cups without lids. Trent sipped, puckered, and gagged.

"Oh," he said, "that's good."

My cup swirled with black liquid and small tan bubbles.

"Go ahead," Trent said. "Try it."

My hand shook a little as I raised the cup to my lips. I thought about Dad and wondered when he first tried coffee. I wondered if maybe this was the first step in my becoming him. Perhaps it all started with a cup of black gas station coffee.

I hesitated, but eventually, I sipped. The warm liquid washed across my jaw and bit my lips. It was bitter. My cheeks puckered and I gagged a little. Trent drove along I-15, sipping his coffee. Despite the taste, I kept drinking and thinking about Dad. And without my realizing it, this was my first step in a long journey of leaving my Mormon faith. And with each step away from Mormonism, I couldn't help but realize that it was one more step in following my dad's example.

I drank only half the cup, and I remember looking over at my older brother as he drove and feeling grateful that our relationship had begun to rekindle. I wondered if we'd have more moments like the one we were having. And naturally, there were a few. A camping trip, a concert here or there. But as the months and years went on, our lives stayed on the same trajectory, Trent doing his thing, while I stayed right there at Grandma's house. He called less and less to tell me about his exciting life outside of Mormonism, and I think it's because he became more engaged in that new, exciting college life and less interested in his old one.

We became comfortable going months without speaking, and sadly this drifting apart from family was something I'd become accustomed to, leaving me with the realization that the only person I could depend on was my grandmother.

ELEPHANT

My junior year, Provo High built a new library. Dad did work on the heating and air-conditioning system. Once, I watched him from a library alcove. I didn't tell him I was there; I just wanted to watch him.

Dad lugged a seven-foot aluminum ladder in his right hand with a sloppy, right-leaning stride, his weary bootheels scraping the carpet. In his left hand was a small plastic cooler. He leaned the ladder against the wall, the rungs scuffed black from his boots, and sat on the floor with his back against a bookshelf. From the cooler he pulled a flat aluminum can of herring and a can of Budweiser nestled in a thin blue insulated can liner. He hunched, his sloping shoulders bent forward, the can of fish between his legs. He gripped chunks of fish with his fingers and chomped them with hard, calloused gums, because he'd lost all of his teeth.

About a year earlier, Dad's teeth blackened and died. He never told me why and at sixteen years old, I didn't know what to make of his missing teeth, but I suspected it had something to do with all the painkillers. That assumption was confirmed years later as I was chatting with a good friend who is a dentist. He was a regular volunteer at the local jail. He told me that one of the more common and tragic parts of his time there was pulling teeth from inmates suffering from drug addiction. "It's not unusual that someone will come in, and they are addicted to painkillers, or heroin, or whatever. They tell me about pain in their mouth, so I take a look, and there really isn't anything in there I can save, and they have to be pulled to prevent an infection. And it's not the drugs that kill the teeth. It's neglect. It's years of bad hygiene and lack of care. It's tragic, really." As he spoke, I couldn't help but think about my dad.

I will say this, though: It was shocking. One day, his teeth were just gone, and his mouth became a soft, meaty cavity with a lonely tongue. Grandma gave him money for dentures, but I don't think he ever got them—and I'm not sure how he spent the money, but naturally I have my suspicions.

Without the reinforcement of teeth, his flesh caved in on the jawbone, giving him this wrinkled kissy-face 24-7. Scrambled eggs, Jell-O, oatmeal, and other soft entrées were his diet. He slurred. His gums bled all the time, causing crud the color of weak strawberry milk to collect in the corners of his mouth. All of it was heartbreaking, sure, but it was also pretty disgusting, and watching him drink a beer and use his hands to eat fish in my high school brought on very real wave of anxiety.

Around this age, I can remember friends complaining to me about how their dad was bald, or how he had a gut, or how he dressed in sagging, discount Sam's Club jeans, or how he wore those nerdy white sneakers all dads wear, which turned green the moment he cut the lawn. My friends talked about how they didn't want to become some middle-aged, worn-out dude with a soul-sucking cubicle job who falls asleep at seven o'clock each night as the family watches a movie. "Not me, man," they would say. "I'm not wasting away like that. I'll never be my dad." And yet, as they lamented about becoming their father, it seemed clear that they knew it was inevitable.

But for me, becoming my dad was a very different fear. It wasn't about one day turning into some dependable yet dorky—but overall lovable—father, like the dude most of my friends had lounging in a recliner on weekends. I was left with the fear that I might end up becoming this toothless, hunched-over, greasy-haired, almost Gollum-like man in Wrangler jeans, eating fish with his hands, not a tooth in his skull. When I looked at my dad, I couldn't help but feel like I was looking through a magical mirror and seeing a glimpse at my dark and depressing future.

And listen, there were similarities.

A lot of them, actually.

I was sixteen years old. Dad wore a size 9 shoe, 32-inch-waist jeans, and a medium shirt. So did I. His handwriting was sloppy and scrunched, lost somewhere between cursive and print. So was mine. In so many ways the two of us were similar: hair and eye color, love for sweets and hatred for spicy foods, irritable stomachs, poor spelling . . .

We both lied all the time too. That was a skill I definitely learned from him. Dad claimed to have slept with his high school math teacher, something I'd never been able to confirm. Not that I ever tried to confirm it, because . . . ew. When he started smoking at forty-three, he told Grandma that the doctor advised he start the habit to help his breathing. When he met his fourth wife, he claimed to have once been a professional bronc rider.

These were lies—I know that now—but he was my dad, and in my early teens I took what he said seriously. There was also evidence to back up his claims. In old photos he looked like a bronco rider in western-style shirts and tight jeans, as slender and muscular as a greyhound with narrow hips and broad shoulders. A doctor could have told him to start smoking—as a youth, I didn't know enough about doctors to ascertain what they would and wouldn't advise a patient to do, although, looking back, this seems about as likely as a doctor advising someone to slam their head in a car door to relieve a headache. And a romantic relationship with his high school math teacher could explain his ability to compute complicated math problems in his head, like how much heating duct a 16,000-square-foot building required.

He read like an unreliable narrator, his dialogue hugging the margins between fact and fiction. I wonder if he liked being more than what he was, and I question if his underhanded lifestyle was something he'd begun doing at a young age or something that started later in his life. Perhaps he had a moment of clarity and realized that his life was not what he'd hoped it would be, so he began redrafting his own past, hopeful that it would influence the future. Not that any of that was working out for him. He was broke, as far as I could tell. Always asking Grandma for money. And most friends and family that knew him usually avoided conversation of, well, him.

It happened all the time. Particularly at church.

Grandma and I went to the same Mormon congregation that Dad grew up in, and he was definitely the elephant in the room. Every time Dad was brought up in casual conversation, and I was around, everyone got quiet. But for me as a teenager, everyone going quiet whenever my dad was brought up made me feel like I was the problem. I had no doubt that if I weren't there, they'd be happy to discuss the ways he'd screwed them out of money, or his divorces, or the times they may have seen him urinating in public, which was a nasty habit he developed around this time.

That silence at the mention of my father made me wonder if *I* was an elephant. If I was the problem. I felt guilty by association, because so many people disliked my dad or didn't agree with his choices. I began to feel like all that silence was directed at me.

While researching this book, I found a list of lawsuits and liens against Dad. It was pretty long, and it included a number of names I recognized. It appeared to tell the story of a man who would take on heating and air-conditioning jobs, get money

ANXiouSLy EVER AFTER

up front, and then never finish the work or do a shoddy job and never come back to repair it.

But of course, I didn't know any of this as a teen. I knew only that he had a bad reputation for burning bridges and odd behavior, and that realization made me assume the worst about him and caused me to feel like a total outcast. I've heard stories of children with famous parents who felt like they would never get out of the shadow of their parents' success. I suppose I felt like I was on the opposite end of that. Like I would never get out of the shadow of my dad's bad behavior.

And yet I couldn't seem to stop mimicking him.

Not that I was going around screwing friends and family out of money. I was a teenager. The best I could do was get a job at Pizza Hut, which I will admit, was a pretty sweet job in high school because I loved pizza. But that love for pizza was the problem, because I stole from the place all the time, which felt like something my dad would have done. On occasion, I claimed I could play Van Halen's "Eruption" guitar solo, which was completely untrue. Not even close. I also sometimes told people I had a really hot girlfriend, and when they asked who, I said, "She goes to another school," which we all know is code for, "I don't have a girlfriend. At all." And sometimes I told people I had once ridden a bull, which is almost comical considering I'd seen numerous bulls in my lifetime but always through a car window because they kinda freaked me out and I was afraid to get out of the car. I compared my dishonesty and theft with my dad's, and I wondered if this was something I was predestined to do.

I longed to be nothing like him. But I couldn't seem to change our similarities, and that fact filled me with absolute dread—a feeling that became very real the moment Dad went to jail for 180 days.

From my understanding, it was a slow building up of petty crimes and forgery that got him locked up.

A year or so before he went to jail, he took me to get a copy of my Social Security card. I was probably fifteen. On the way, we stopped at a doctor's office because Dad had an appointment. I sat in the lobby doing homework when the doctor came out. He was a tall and slender white man with brown hair. He was wearing blue scrubs. He was clearly flustered, his face red. He gave the receptionist a sticky note in this jerking motion, almost like he was going to hit her with it. I couldn't see her too well. She was sitting behind one of those tall check-in counters. He stated that she was not to give this man another appointment. He said, "This guy's crazy," and that he was "seeking drugs" and he wanted "nothing to do with him."

"I told you about him already, and I'm not sure how he was allowed to have another appointment." Then he paused, made eye contact with me, and bit his tongue. He got quiet, and once again, I was the elephant in the room.

The receptionist said she was sorry, that it wouldn't happen again. Then she asked if she needed to call the police.

"No," he said. "Not this time."

Then he walked away.

Dad came out wearing this flat-lipped look. As he was giving the woman his information, I hopped a little, pulled myself over that tall counter, and peeked at the woman's desk. Dad's name was written on the sticky note, and I felt absolute terror reading it. I knew his name was going to be on it, but I hoped that I was wrong. I wanted to be wrong so bad, but when my suspicion was confirmed, my stomach dropped.

And you know, when I think back on this moment, I can't understand why this doctor didn't offer Dad help. Why didn't he recommend some sort of rehab? And maybe he did, but from my angle, it looked like he was just pushing Dad away.

We went to two other clinics that day, until Dad finally found someone willing to write him a prescription for painkillers.

What I didn't realize at the time was that other doctors in the area were catching on to Dad. He was traveling farther and farther to find someone willing to prescribe to him, so his solution was to start making his own prescriptions.

The same move Dad pulled with child support checks years earlier he tried pulling with prescriptions for pain medications. He'd go from one doctor to another, get paper prescriptions for pain meds, and then make copies on a Xerox machine.

He took copies to various pharmacies around town. I don't know all the details, but I can imagine him in a polyester shirt with three open buttons,

Wrangler jeans, and boots, with a gold chain around his neck, sliding a clumsily cut and xeroxed prescription across the pharmacy counter, a watermark reading "Copy" clearly visible, and then casually winking at the attractive twenty-something pharmacy tech, giving her a cocky grin that fifteen years earlier may have sealed the deal. But by this time in his life, he didn't have any teeth, making the whole scene tragic.

Then there were the many times he was caught driving while intoxicated. Eventually, it all added up and he was sent to jail for 180 days.

The day Dad was sentenced, Grandma went through her pink and turquoise address book and called family. Then she called friends. This was strange behavior for her. Mornings she made her bed, afternoons she vacuumed the carpet, and evenings she handwashed dishes. She silently baked bread and pulled weeds. She was a reserved and domestic Mormon widow who watched *The Lawrence Welk Show*, *Matlock*, and *Diagnosis Murder* rather than new shows with new actors who might offend her. She was not a gossip. But most of that day, she sat at her yellow rotary phone, the same phone Bell began renting to her decades earlier when they installed the line, telling the same story. "He's got himself locked up . . . for drinking while driving . . . I don't know what I'm gonna do." Once the phone calls were exhausted, Grandma sat in her white vinyl rocker, swaying back and forth, the ball bearing hinges rolling and popping.

She never told me directly that my dad was a fool, with no direction and little common sense. And she never asked me what she could have done differently or how she should feel, or if it was her fault or his. But I overheard all of these questions with each phone call.

For several days she called friends and family and then sat in her rocker, hands across her lap. She never discovered anything new, but I think it felt good to have someone other than me to talk to. Someone to say, "I understand," even though they probably didn't. I watched from the hallway as Grandma sat in her rocker, her anxious toes moving inside small white shoes as she held the phone to her ear. Perhaps what she was waiting to hear was, "It's not your fault."

I don't know if anyone told her that.

If I were to describe one emotion I could feel from her, it was anxiety. She was anxious to the bone about this. It was at the top of her mind and in the tips of her fingers. It was in her small trembling knees and the way she rubbed her hands across her face, and I couldn't help but look at her and realize that we were both feeling the same tightness in our stomachs about Dad being in jail.

As crazy as this may sound, however, Dad's time in jail was probably the most consistent—and dare I say best—relationship I ever had with him.

His phone calls, his visitors, his life, were all regulated. Sometimes he called my brother, who was twenty years old and living just outside Salt Lake City. And sometimes he called his last wife.

But most of the time, he called Grandma and me.

The Utah County Jail was thirty minutes from Grandma's house. Grandma's vision was bad enough that she couldn't drive anymore, so I drove her every Thursday. The first time we visited, Grandma didn't ask that I turn on my blinker, or slow down, or not drive so dang close to the curb. She didn't speak at all. Her eyes were fixed on the highway leading us from Dad's childhood home to the cell he now lived in.

Each cellblock of the Utah County Jail is named after a ski resort—Alta, Solitude, Snowbird, and Sundance. We met Dad in the Solitude corridor, and it was stagnant and dry and not what I'd expected. I was a teen, and I didn't understand the distinction between prison and jail. It was also cleaner than I expected. And so very, very quiet.

Dad sat with his arms crossed reverently, wearing a white crew neck T-shirt that was visible through the V-neck of an orange jumpsuit. Boyish heartbreaking freckles spackled his cheekbones and contrasted with his small-pitted eyes and dark eyebrows. We always sat on either side of bullet-proof glass, and we spoke using these big heavy phones that were attached with steel cables.

Whenever Grandma and I visited Dad in jail, he wasn't completely sober. Most of his addictions were prescription medications, so he was allowed to still have some of them. But he was more sober than I'd seen him in years, and in a lot of ways he seemed very reflective. The receiver crackled, flattening his usual chirp to the husky baritone of a longtime smoker. His face showed a mix of fear and boredom, his eyes were glossy and cold, and at times I couldn't tell if he was looking at us or a reflection in the glass.

Sometimes he asked me about school or my job at Pizza Hut. Other times, he asked me about how Grandma was keeping up. Our conversations were surface level, and my visits consisted mostly of long stretches of silence—we just sat, the phone line crackling, as I took in the fact that I was there, talking to my father in jail, while he was clearly thinking about his life and how he ended up living in a jail cell.

Once, after we visited Dad, Grandma stirred warm milk with a wooden spoon at two o'clock in the morning. She wore a pink nightgown with matching slippers, hair in a faded green headscarf protecting her perm. I sat at the bar and she said, "I wish there was something I could do." And what I think she wanted to say was, "I wish there was something I could have done." Then she let out a long breath and her shoulders slumped, her body tired with age and stress, and said with her back still to me, her voice just above a whisper, "I pray every day that I'm doing right by you. I don't ever want to see you in a mess like this."

And she was right. He was a mess of a man, her youngest son, and in that moment it seemed clear that although taking me in at her age was obviously a hardship, she did it because she saw it as a way to raise me right, because she believed she'd done such a poor job with my father.

And while that seems altruistic of her—and in so many ways she really did save my life by taking me into her home—the realization that raising me was some amends for the way my father turned out weighted me with guilt, like raising me was a burden I was born to become. And that guilt, combined with my fear that I might turn into that man living in jail, fed my anxiety. But like I was so accustomed to doing, I never told anyone about how I felt, not even Grandma, and all of these feelings and realizations made me once again feel like I was the elephant in the room.

After the PE poop situation, Grandma had become a real confidant when it came to my struggles with anxiety. She would talk me down. Sometimes she would just look at me, grip my forearm in the sweetest and most loving way possible, and say, "Honey, you're anxious. You need to breathe a little." And those simple phrases were wonderful, because she was the only person I felt comfortable speaking with about my anxiety.

At the same time, I was a boy, soon to be a man, and I felt like I was supposed to be stronger than this. But I wasn't, and I felt a deep fear of being judged or criticized for the emotions I couldn't control. Being able to talk to Grandma about those troubled feelings was a lifeline.

I could see her struggle with the burden of my dad sitting in jail. And I loved her too much to add to that burden with my own feelings, so I bottled them up, and doing so only made me feel alone and more anxious and in a lot of ways led to my first real feelings of depression.

We visited Dad the week before his release. I watched Grandma as she spoke with Dad. Struggling to make out his words, she pushed the phone hard against her ear. I could see Dad's face and shoulders. Grandma replied in curt yeses and nos, sometimes silently nodding. Dad spoke while moving his hands, and between words the muscles of his jaw flexed. Both stopped for a moment, and Dad mouthed, "I'm sorry."

Dad didn't apologize after he cheated on my mother, or after he showed up to my parent-teacher conference unannounced and drunk, or after Grandma confronted him about his leaving his faith. But on the other side of the glass, across from Grandma, he apologized again, and again. After the third time, both stopped, and in their silence, I assumed this was the first time Grandma had heard him apologize. She cried in somber, simple tears that suggested reconciliation and relief.

Dad and I spoke next. He rubbed the phone with his palm, hand thin and spiderlike, jaw moving from side to side, tongue mindlessly searching for teeth like the mussel of a clam searching for a lost pearl. Everything about him suggested fatigue. His eyes were moist with longing, knuckles white and cracking, shoulders slumped and weary. Dad dragged a dry tongue across his lips and said, "I don't want to see you in here. Ever. You don't have to—you know that. You're the good one." He stopped for a moment, let out a breath, and said something that gave me pause, "Better than me."

The setting was terrible. I don't think anyone wants to visit their father in jail. But there was a freeing feeling in Dad's advice. It felt like he was looking back at his own mistakes and comparing them to my life and realizing that I had the opportunity to become more. And for a scared teenage boy with a drug-addicted father, struggling to understand his own mental illness and being raised by his grandmother, what my father said ended up charging me with optimism and was ultimately the best advice he ever gave me.

PART 2

OBSESSIVE-COMPULSIVE DISORDER

I HAVE NO PLANS.
NOT A SINGLE ONE.

I was seventeen, turning eighteen in a couple of months. I'd just finished high school, and I was chatting with my boss at Pizza Hut. He asked what I was going to do now that school was over, and I said, "I'm taking a year off before college."

But that was a lie.

I had no plans.

Not a single one.

James happened to be my former Mormon young men's leader in addition to being my boss at Pizza Hut. He was a relatively short and stocky man, a father of five or six kids (I'd lost count), and he had dark brown hair and large brown eyes. According to him, in his youth he looked a lot like Matthew Broderick. He brought that up from time to time. Okay . . . he brought it up a lot. In fact, his claim to fame was that, as a teenager, he once sang "Twist and Shout" at a parade dressed in a white shirt and a cheetah-print vest, just like in *Ferris Bueller's Day Off*.

What I'm getting at is that if you can imagine a middle-aged Ferris Bueller managing a Pizza

Hut, wearing black slacks with matching slip-resistant shoes and a white apron with pizza sauce smeared across it, then you can imagine what it was like working for James. He was a thoughtful, kind man who often invited me to his home for dinner, and sometimes he paid me in free pizza coupons to clean his minivan, which was always an eye-opening preview into the realities of exactly how much kids don't give a crap about a minivan.

I absolutely envied his children. That was a straight fact. Sure, they were much younger than me, but they really had that happy Mormon family thing going on. From what I could tell, James was a stand-up dad, and I assumed he'd always been a stand-up guy. The kind of guy that would, at any given moment, drop to the floor for a wrestling match with his son, or break into a dorky Batman voice until his throat gave out, or pretend to be a *Spider-Man* villain, or kiss a hurt knee in the middle of a dinner conversation. I couldn't help thinking to myself, *This is it. This is exactly what I wish I had.* And all of it caused me to have mixed feelings while visiting his home.

Part of me just wanted to sit there and soak it in, but there was also an equally strong emotion, a darker, envious emotion that I think all kids from dysfunctional homes feel: I'd look at a happy family and think, *Screw this noise! What made these kids so special to get good parents?*

I'd chew on that envy every time I visited James.

Having a family like his, whether that be as a child or a father, felt about as likely as going to Mars, or swimming across the ocean, or suddenly becoming emotionally stable enough to *not* have to consider exactly how far away I was from a restroom at any given time so I didn't crap my pants—again. And I think the belief that I'd never have a stable family was part of the reason I stopped attending church in my late teens. Mormonism is all about happy families, and moms and dads, and these relationships that are supposed to linger into eternity, forever and ever.

And holy crap!

All that sounded absolutely terrible for me.

No lie.

Honestly, I couldn't imagine how painful it would be to spend eternity with my parents. And I know that sounds harsh, but sadly, it was true. And not for the typical teenager "They make me take a shower and follow a curfew" or "My dad is into *Star Wars* and wears New Balance sneakers" reasons my other friends often complained about. The only family member I felt comfortable spending eternity with was my grandmother. The rest, well, at that age, after all the arguments, and fires, and drugs, and anxiety crawling from my stomach and up into my neck whenever they were around . . . Frankly, I didn't like the idea of spending an afternoon with those people, let alone eternity.

I don't want to point out the obvious, but eternity lasts *forever*. And that's a really long time.

ANXIOUSLY EVER AFTER

There was also the fact that family seemed so temporary to me. By this time, my mother had remarried. This was her third marriage, and like with my father's marriages, I was not invited to the wedding. Dad was in the middle of another divorce. I think it was his fourth. By the time I graduated high school, I had a slew of stepsiblings, half siblings, former grandparents, stepcousins . . . I could go on, but you get the idea. I didn't even have names for some of these relationships. I stopped trying to get to know people I was related to. Family came in and out of my life like customers entering and exiting a department store, so what was the point?

For me, family wasn't something that lasted for eternity, like Mormonism said, and I didn't want it to.

Family was something that lasted until two people got tired of each other and got divorced, and I had absolutely no control over any of that. The constant movement, all of that loose footing when it came down to people I could depend on, made me feel like I had only one person who was in my corner consistently, and that was Grandma. And she was getting older. At this time, I wasn't sure how old she was, probably in her late seventies—but at seventeen years old, I felt like she was somewhere between 80 and the distance from Earth to the sun. I knew it was only a matter of time before she would pass on, and I'd have absolutely no one to turn to.

And that reality was terrifying.

But what was even more frightening was the notion that I could somehow figure out life and become a decent father and husband like James. It was unfathomable, and feeling like a happy and stable family was unobtainable gave me conflicting feelings about going to church and singing songs about families being eternal and trying to act like that was actually an option for me.

Because it wasn't.

But James, bless his heart, was not the kind of man to give up on one of his young men. And when I started getting lukewarm with the Mormon church, and started letting my hair grow out, and started hanging out with more and more of those other long-haired crum-bums who, like me, had no real plans for college or a family, he called and offered me a job at Pizza Hut. And I accepted, even though it seemed clear that he was doing this only as a way to keep in touch with me since I wasn't going to church anymore. But hey, when you're a crum-bum with greasy long hair and a wallet chain that began as a choke chain for a dog, getting a part-time job isn't easy in a staunchly Mormon town.

So I was pretty grateful.

But now, high school was over, and James had been promoted and was going to move to another part of the state, where he'd be managing multiple stores.

I knew a few kids who actually went off to college, but I wasn't friends with those kids. They came from nice families, with married parents who went to college. Families a lot like James's. Those kids' parents told them not to hang around kids like me. That was a fact. And it's not that I was necessarily a bad kid. I just came from a checkered family, and that was enough to blacklist me from most families' dinner tables. James, however, always invited me to his home, even when other families wouldn't.

I didn't always accept his invitations for the reasons listed earlier, but I always appreciated the thought behind them.

Anyway, on James's last day at the restaurant, he pulled me into the back storage area and asked me what my plans were after high school, and I told him what I'd been telling everyone since I returned my rented cap and gown: "I'm going to take a year off before college."

Or at least that's what I thought I was doing. It's not like I had college in mind at any time during high school. I didn't take the ACT or SAT. I didn't even know what those tests were. I barely graduated high school. I never learned how to type, and I'd never finished reading a novel. If I were to try to place my reading level, it was easily somewhere between *Where the Wild Things Are* and having enough gumption to read the first couple chapters of *Harry Potter and the Sorcerer's Stone* but never finishing it. I was the kind of kid who got his English and math credits in remedial classes and filled in the rest with shop courses. Not that I was particularly good at working with my hands. I wasn't. I actually set fire to my pants more times than I successfully produced a respectable arc weld, and the dresser I took a full year to make earned me a solid C minus in Intermediate Woodworking. I was no craftsman. But shop was where all the crum-bums tended to be placed, so I felt at home next to a band saw but never all that comfortable actually using the band saw. I was a C student in shop classes and a C student in remedial classes, and none of this qualified me for Harvard or even the state university—not that I knew the difference between the two.

When I first moved in with Grandma, I stopped turning in assignments. I was still missing a lot of school because of anxiety-related stomach pains, and I had a hard time concentrating in school because I was, you know, anxious all the time. My personal life was a mess. Educators, church members, the whole tamale wanted me to overcome all that crap and become the valedictorian.

They all wanted me to become the feel-good story of the year.

But when things went to crap with my family, that fear, those emotions, the worry, the anxiety, all of it still sat in my stomach—even after I'd found a safe and calm home at Grandma's—every moment I tried to calm myself just long enough to pay attention in class. My anxiety sat next to me on the school bus. It was inside my backpack, and waiting in my locker. It was always on my shoulder and in my pocket. It followed me everywhere.

Anxiety took over my thoughts the moment I tried to focus on a homework assignment or read a book, causing me to be able to concentrate on only one thing: my anxiety, my fear. Just getting Cs and Ds in a couple of courses was emotionally exhausting. I was asked pretty regularly, "Why aren't you paying attention?" and, "Why are you failing?" And the answer to the questions seemed so obvious: "My life's a mess. I can't focus on anything else because I'm scared all the time." But unfortunately, there was no excuse for bad grades, so I looked for friends like me, who had similar lives and challenges, because at least they could understand my hardship—and naturally, once we all got into a room together, we were described as crum-bums, which really only furthered my commitment to the status.

That conversation with my father in jail, though—when he said I could become more than him—had more of an impact than I ever could have hoped. Sure, I barely graduated high school. I failed most of my classes my freshman and sophomore years, but after what Dad said, my friends started dropping out, and I started turning it on. I became more focused than ever before, and I ended up doing four years of high school in two. It wasn't pretty, sure. My transcript was a mess. But I graduated, and even got an award for most improved student.

But like James, everyone was now asking me about my post-graduation plans, while I was trying to lick my wounds from the past four years. I was still living with my grandmother. I graduated at seventeen because I have an August birthday, not because I skipped a grade or anything. My head was a mess, my anxiety was ever present, and the thought of trying to plan for the future when I was still trying to make sense of my past was exhausting.

Graduation felt like I'd just jumped off a cliff.

So yeah, I had zero plans.

Nada.

Nothing.

But I didn't know how to tell people that, and they didn't want to hear it, so I gave them the same cookie-cutter answer I gave James. "I'm taking a year off before going to college."

It sounded good. People nodded. Basically, it was my way of telling friends, family, even myself to leave me alone without saying, "Leave me alone as I try to find a path that doesn't include becoming addicted to drugs or serving jail time, like my father." But in reality I had no idea how to be more than my dad. And sadly, when your dad's a mess, most people assume you're going to become a mess too. It's that old idiom about the apple not falling far from the tree. And sure, they didn't say that outright, and each time I said, "I'm taking a year off and then going to college," people left me alone. But there was something in their eyes, something behind the way they said, "Sure, sure . . ." that really said, "Looks like you're following in Daddy's footsteps."

But James, he was different. I stood across from him in the same black slacks and slip-resistant shoes we all wore. Only my slacks sagged well

below my hips, causing me to walk on the back of
the pant legs. My hair was down to my shoulders,
and I sported this spindly goatee. My Pizza Hut
hat was on backward, and pimples gobbled up my
chin and forehead. He looked me in the eyes after I
said I was taking a year off before college. He put
his hand on my shoulder, smiled, and said, "I don't
believe you for a moment."

It was quiet. I could hear the other cooks
working in the kitchen. I didn't know exactly what
to say. I didn't expect him to see through me like
that, but after being my boss for more than a year,
he easily knew me.

I didn't respond, and after a moment of silence,
he said, "I don't think you have any plans. To tell
ya the truth, I don't know if you ever have. But
you know what, I don't know if I did at your age
either."

Then he told me this story about when he
was my age and people kept asking him what he
was going to do. He didn't know, so he decided
to go on a two-year Mormon mission, something
I'd already declined to do. He met a woman while
there, and they fell in love. "Or at least I thought
it was love," he said, chuckling to himself. "It was
more lust than love." He looked me in the eyes and
said, "There's a difference. Trust me."

They became intimate, and he got sent home
from his mission. This whole story—from the
mission to the sex—was scandalous, but it was
also a huge taboo for a Mormon missionary.

I stood there in complete shock.

He told me he flew home and didn't even leave the airport. He got on the next flight back, and the two got married. But it didn't last very long. Maybe a year. "It was a really bad relationship. All of it was a bad decision looking back now." He looked at the ground for a moment with those big brown eyes. He twisted his lips to the side, and then said, "We were too young, and it went bad so very fast. And when it was all over, I was depressed. It took me a number of years to get my life back together. I eventually went to college and married someone I really love. And now we have kids that are pretty great."

He shrugged, and I remember pausing, looking at this man that had exactly what I'd always wished for: a calm, intact family. He was happily married. He seemed like a really good dad and an all-around nice guy. And yet he'd been sent home from his mission and had been through a divorce I'd never known about. It felt like I'd finally seen the seams in his concrete. He'd made mistakes and overcome them, and knowing that, well, it gave me a lot of hope.

"Having plans at your age is kind of a scam," he said. "So don't feel too bad. You're going to figure it out. I know that much. You're a nice kid, you've just had some bad luck. But I believe in you enough to know that you're going to be okay. Just give it a little time."

Then he gave me a heartfelt hug, and I felt a surge of relief.

Someone had finally told me a very simple

ANXIOUSLY EVER AFTER

truth. Sometimes things get bad, but they can still work out. And as crazy as this may sound, I'd never heard anything like that before. Or maybe someone had said it, but I wasn't listening. I did that a lot as a teenager. But I was listening now. James became the first person I'd ever met who'd made some mistakes but then was able to figure it out and made a good life for himself.

I'd seen people from good families go on to have good families and success. And I'd known people like me, who had complicated families and had gone on to make things more complicated. But knowing that James had made some mistakes and that he was still able to make life work, well, it was pretty good for me to hear, particularly on the eve of what was soon to become one of the darkest times of my life.

DRUGS AT
A TOY STORE

I left Pizza Hut in the fall of 2000 for a night job stocking shelves at a large toy store. Which I thought would be a fun place to work, because, you know, it was a toy store. I mean, who doesn't love a toy store? I don't know, the devil probably, because he likes only misery and sadness and finding new ways to create really irritating YouTube celebrities. But not me—I loved toy stores. This place was the Home Depot of toys. It was where I went to get every birthday gift until the age of fifteen. I longed to go there as a child. Wall-to-wall joy, with a mascot and everything. But let me make something very clear: At night, after the customers had left, this toy store became a shockingly awesome place to score drugs.

The night staff had two populations. There were college students from Brigham Young University. They pretty much kept to themselves. The rest were predominantly seasonal workers from the local carnival. When they got laid off for the winter, they'd get jobs stocking shelves at night for the Christmas rush. I have to assume this was a pretty standard trajectory for most winter seasonal jobs around Utah County. But as a Mormon kid from Provo, I quickly realized that these were some of the roughest people I'd ever encountered.

Now, full confession. In high school, I smoked pot a couple times a week for about six months. Maybe less. I got in with these two heavy pot smokers. I can't even remember their names now, but I want to say one went by Jimbo or Bubba, and the other was a Tyler of some sort. They were skateboarding hippie dudes. You know, the guys that were into Pink Floyd and The Grateful Dead, with divorced parents, same as mine. Their dads weren't really around either, and I guess I felt like we were similar in that way. Like our home lives were equally crummy and we could bond over that. We all had long hair, and baggy '90s jeans with wallet chains and skate shoes. Most of our shirts were from concerts.

We'd hang out at the school tennis court, smoke a bowl or two, and then wander over to the grocery store for off-brand Mountain Dew and discount Little Debbie cookies. We'd stuff our faces in the parking structure of a nearby apartment complex, cutting class, and snort-laughing, and discussing how everyone was a hypocrite and school was created by communists (as if we even knew what a communist was). "People need to free the green," Jimbo would say. "And blah, blah, blah. Screw the system. Blah, blah, blah. That cloud looks like the Death Star." At the time, I thought I was pretty hard-core and cool, but in reality I was just a pimple-faced short kid in a complicated on-again, off-again relationship with deodorant.

It was around this time that Dad started showing up for work on that new school library. One morning, I ran into him after smoking pot with Jimbo and Tyler. He was in the parking lot getting some tools from his truck. We were cutting class and we were all pretty high, and for some strange pot-minded reason, I thought it would be funny to ask my dad to smile so my new stoner buddies could see that he didn't have any teeth. Which, I will say, wasn't funny at all—it was disrespectful to my dad, who was clearly going through some things.

Anyway, Dad gave me this eye roll, then wrestled his face into a toothless, black-gummed grin, stuck out his tongue, and said, "Blahhh." He couldn't have weighed more than 100 pounds, his skull pushing against his skin like a stone near the surface of a river, his baggy jeans clinging to his hips with a tightly drawn cowboy belt.

I laughed long and hard, a hand over my stomach. In so many ways, I was trying to laugh at my situation, my life, the pain of it all. Dad giggled a little with me, and then turned around and went back to what he was doing. I looked at my friends and quickly realized I was the only one laughing. We walked a little ways from my dad, and then Jimbo said, "Dang, dude, your dad looks pretty messed up."

Tyler nodded.

At this time, I didn't fully understand what my dad was into. I knew he wasn't well, and I suspected he took too many pain pills, but he was adamant that he was sick. All of his prescriptions were from a doctor, which seemed to legitimize what he was doing, even though I knew he was shopping for doctors. Most of my teen years, I wavered between *My dad has a legitimate illness* and *My dad is a drug addict.*

But suddenly I was with these dudes who I thought were tough and cool because they had a pot connection, and I assumed they had lives pretty similar to mine because their parents were divorced—and here they were, looking at me with complete empathy because of my dad. Tyler even said, "I'm sorry about your dad, dude. He's got problems." Suddenly I felt very low and scared, and this was the last time I smoked pot.

And I bring this up because by the time I got that job at the toy store, those few months smoking pot was the most experience I'd ever had with recreational drugs until a coworker pulled me into the breakroom and asked, "Wanna buy some pills?"

He was a short kid with dark hair and a slight overbite. We went to rival high schools, so we knew some of the same people, and all those kids were pretty heavy drug users. He clearly assumed I also was a heavy drug user. It was one of those guilty-by-association things. I told him, "No, man. I'm good."

He shrugged, and then walked away.

153

This was the moment I started to realize most of my coworkers were heavy drug users, and they assumed I was too. And to be fair, I looked a lot like these dudes, with my shoulder-length hair, the bottom half bleached Crayola yellow, the top half my natural brown, all of it greasy and split at the ends. I had the massive-legged, rave-style JNCO jeans, and I was trying to grow a beard—but I was eighteen and it grew only from my neck, giving me this Amish vibe. I'd love to blame my look on the '90s and the nu metal craze. But this was 2000, and the baggy-pants raver look was already going out of fashion, so this really was on me.

The guy I was assigned to stock shelves with went by Million-Dollar, or just Millions for short. I don't remember his real name, but I do remember that he was quite tall, well over six foot, and impossibly thin. He was an aspiring DJ who each night wore the same pair of soiled massive-legged JNCO jeans and scuffed white Adidas shoes with nearly paper-thin soles. He liked to talk about how he'd killed people, but his outlandish descriptions of murder were sketchy at best.

He said things like, "It was a dozen people, man. Blood was all over the floor. I stepped in it and it felt like sticky melted chocolate." Then he'd quiet down to almost a whisper, his eyes looking left and right, up and down, almost like the cops were listening, and say, "I can't believe I got away with killing all those people." And everyone in the breakroom would just nod, and say, "Sure, Millions. Sure, you did." When he wasn't talking about killing people, he'd talk about all the girls he'd slept with. Thousands by his count. The song "Pretty Fly (for a White Guy)" by The Offspring was popular that year, and it kinda felt like I was working with the protagonist from the rock video. You know, if the guy in the video also talked about killing people.

But what was undeniable was how often he went into the breakroom with the guy who offered me pain pills. They'd speak quietly. Then they'd each pass the other something.

It wasn't hard to figure out what was going on.

By November, I'd turned down more drugs working at the toy store than at any point in my life. But it was the painkillers being passed around that gave me the most pause. I'd seen my fair share of prescription pain pills by this point because of my dad. But I'd never taken any except for one or two when my wisdom teeth were removed. I was scared of them, and for good reason. Some primal part of me knew that they were dangerous because of what I'd witnessed. But the fact that they were usually prescribed by a doctor and distributed at a pharmacy made them seem safe. Almost like they were harmless, or even healthy, as long as they had been prescribed by a doctor.

All these other drugs I was hearing about at the toy store, the heroin, and the cocaine, and the pot—those drugs were illegal. Those were the really scary drugs, the bad drugs, the ones that would ruin your life, according to every single teacher and police officer I'd ever encountered. They were the subject of the War on Drugs. I was watching my dad evaporate from prescription pill abuse, and yet I still—to some extent—bought into the safety of prescription pills. Looking back now, I wonder if I just wanted to believe that they were safe. I wanted to believe that Dad had some physical ailment, like he claimed, because it was easier to admit to that than to fully own that he was addicted.

But hearing Vicodin, Percocet, OxyContin—all the brand names I recognized from my father's medicine cabinet—being discussed at work with the same gusto as heroin and other hard illegal drugs really shook me.

And all of it made me think back to that time when my brother and I found Dad passed out in his truck from an overdose.

As Dad was sleeping in the hospital and I was in the waiting room, my brother came in and said he spoke with Dad's wife over the phone. This was the same woman Dad had left my mother for. She told Trent that Dad needed to go to rehab, and we both looked at each other, trying to figure out what that even meant. We were these teenage kids, living in Utah County and raised Mormon.

"Rehab?" I asked. "What's that?"

Both of us were baffled, not sure what she was talking about but afraid to ask any questions of the doctors because we assumed doing so would make us look stupid.

It wasn't until years later that I realized she was saying Dad needed a drug rehabilitation program because he was addicted. I'd pushed that conversation out of my mind until my job at the toy store.

By this time, Dad was out of jail and living in a small apartment in American Fork, Utah. He was still in Utah County, and his place was probably a twenty-minute drive from my grandmother's house, where I was still living. Although I didn't realize it at the time, this was the evening of his life. I could see it in the way his cheekbones pushed against his skin. I could see it in his thin, greasy, graying hair and the nicotine yellow in the whites of his eyes. I could see it in his trembling spiderlike legs and matching bony fingers.

After being released, Dad got a job at Jameson Heating and Air-Conditioning. I later found out this was a place owned by a guy my dad knew before I was born. They were old friends, so despite Dad's criminal record and bad reputation, the owner gave him a job building heating ducts. I can only imagine how difficult it was for the owner of this shop to eventually fire Dad. Although I never knew the official reason for his termination, I heard a rumor that he was fired for selling prescription pills to coworkers.

I remember visiting Dad with Grandma, and she asked him about his job and what we'd heard. And naturally, he said he was innocent, just like he claimed to have never cheated on my mother, or to have never shopped doctors to find prescriptions, or to have never driven while intoxicated. There was always a crappy cop with a chip on his shoulder, or an accusatory jerk who Dad had pissed off back in the day, or a flirtatious waitress who needed a ride and Dad's good intentions created a misunderstanding. Grandma rarely called him on his lies, which was out of character for her.

By this stage in our relationship, it was common for Grandma to look me squarely in the face and call me a "lying idiot." Then she'd take a breath and say something maternal. "You don't need to lie to your grandmother. She loves you too much to be lied to."

I think it was her age. I just didn't feel good about lying to a sweet little old lady. But it was also how much she meant to me. It felt like she had a power or was using a magic spell. It was always the same: She'd say the preceding and then begin to nod, and I'd find myself nodding along with her and then give her the truth, and nothing but the truth.

Then she'd pat my leg, and say, "Don't you feel better now that you've told your grandma what's really going on?"

I'd nod again, and then she'd begin a lecture.

But with Dad, it was different.

I think she wanted his lies to be true. No one felt more obligated to grant Dad the benefit of the doubt than Grandma. Dad said he needed money for rent or gas or groceries, but regardless of how much money Grandma gave him, his eyes were always glossy, the rent was always overdue, his Ford pickup was always one notch above empty, and his fridge and cupboards were always bare. But the medicine cabinet, that was a different story.

It was always, without a doubt, full of bottles. Grandma must have known that her money was going to some other purpose, something she didn't agree with, but she always gave it to him because I think she liked believing that he could spend it on gas. Like Grandma, I also preferred to accept his lies. He asked me for money, and I gave it to him for the same reasons Grandma did.

I visited Dad every other week, always at 7:00 p.m., before my 9:00 p.m. shift at the toy store. Sometimes I brought Grandma. He hadn't been in a relationship that I knew about since he divorced his fourth wife. None of his ex-wives wanted anything to do with him. For the most part, he'd burned every partner he'd ever had. No friends stopped by. Grandma and I were his only visitors.

He'd often tell me there were people living in his attic, and he'd ask me to go up there with him and check. We'd work our way into a small crawl space above his house with an old ladder he used when he was doing heating and air-conditioning work. We'd move around in there, hunched over, lighting the darkness with flashlights. I never saw any evidence in that attic to prove what he was hearing. We'd get out of the attic, put the ladder away, and by the time we'd made it back into the kitchen, he'd stop and say, "Shhh . . . Be quiet." He'd cup his ear with his hand and say, "Can you hear them? They're talking again."

"No, Dad," I'd say. "I don't hear a thing."

The fact that Grandma and I were Dad's only visitors was for the best, considering he sometimes came to the door confused and wearing nothing but stained briefs. He'd do this comical body jerk when I told him to get dressed, almost like he was as shocked to see himself undressed as I was. I'd pull him into the house, ask him to put pants back on, and then he'd tell me how I dressed like a girl.

He'd comment on my baggy jeans and pull on my sad prepubescent beard and say, "I've got a razor in the bathroom you could use." And as odd as it was to hear him comment on my clothing after he'd just come to the door in his underwear, I must admit that I kind of looked forward to these moments when he hassled me to dress better, shave my face, get a haircut. It felt like he was trying to be a dad, which was a feeling I longed for, and I think these moments kept me visiting him.

Grandma would go on about how both of us needed to learn how to "dress proper." Then she'd sit in one of Dad's stained secondhand living room chairs, her hand over her forehead, looking at my dad with an expression that can be described only as personal failure. I could tell that she didn't know what to do with my father.

But to be fair, I don't think anyone did, including Dad.

I don't know what a decade-plus of heavy prescription drug abuse does to someone, but what I can say is that he was toothless and frail, confused and scared, broke and tired. He was hearing voices, and he kept all of his things in cardboard boxes, because he knew it was just a matter of time before he'd be evicted for not paying rent. I asked him on multiple occasions if he really needed all these prescriptions, and he'd dive into the same old script, telling me he was sick. Then he'd shake one of his prescription bottles and say, "See? It's from a doctor, ya idiot."

But his illness, it always changed. Sometimes he had another ulcer. Sometimes he had a hernia. For a while he had something called polyneuropathy. At one point, he said he had cancer. He always had something that caused pain. Something that required more pain pills. One thing was undeniable. My dad was ill, but the real lingering question was whether it was a long-term, chronically painful illness, like he claimed, or an addiction. Looking back now, I can see it was both, because addiction is an illness, and I think one of my biggest regrets is continuing to lie to myself about his addictions and not trying to help him find some sort of rehab program.

In November, Grandma had a stroke, and suddenly I was Dad's only visitor.

It happened in the afternoon, while I was asleep. When I woke up, I got a call from my aunt explaining the situation. Grandma was in the hospital, recovering as best as she could, but it seemed clear that she'd never really be the same again. The stroke took most of her vision and the coordination of her right arm and leg. Her speech was slower than it used to be, drawn out at times as she struggled to find the right words, and she often slurred as she spoke. I remember visiting her in the hospital instead of sleeping, half awake and sitting across from her, exhausted and yet unable to leave her side because I was terrified I might lose her. She'd always appeared to be 800 years old to me as a teenager, but at this moment, in the hospital, after her stroke, she looked 20 years older—her face sagging, drool pooling below her chin, her body tired and frail and ready to call it a day.

She spent close to a week in the hospital. Then she was moved to a care facility. I'd visit her every day after work, at 6:00 a.m. She shared a room with another elderly woman who would yell at me for visiting too early. "Can't you come by at a decent time?" she'd ask. "People sleep around here!"

And to be fair, I *did* visit outside of normal visiting hours. However, with my work schedule, I was given special permission to visit early in the mornings.

The woman would eventually tell me I dressed like an idiot, and then tell Grandma to tell me to get a haircut and some pants that fit properly.

Grandma would be lying in an elevated bed, yelling at her while shaking her good hand, her voice still slurred, the words as wet and sloshy as a rain gutter, "Oh, shut up, you old witch!"

Only she didn't say *witch*.

I'd never heard my staunchly Mormon grandmother use language like that, but there was something about the stroke that seemed to have loosened her tongue a little.

The roommate would yell back, and Grandma would holler more insults, peppered with some swears. Eventually the woman would turn to her side, so her back was to us, and pull the blanket over her head. I'm not sure what their relationship was like during the day, but in the mornings when I visited, it felt a lot like a real-life production of *The Golden Girls*.

Sure enough, once the argument was over and the woman had turned her back to us, Grandma would grip my hand and kindly ask me in a whisper to get a haircut and offer to buy me some pants that fit.

There is something about working nights that caused everything in my life to become a blur of night and day. When Grandma was in the hospital and I thought I was going to lose her, I was up a lot during the day. Then I went to work on only a couple hours of sleep. At the same time, I was watching my father tragically kill himself with prescription pills. And with all the drugs being passed around at my work, I was starting to fully realize what my dad was into. Grandma, the one person I felt I could depend on, wasn't going to be around much longer. That fact seemed very clear to me as I watched her slowly hobble around, a cane in her left hand, struggling to see. She was so far from the tough woman who once shooed a drunk man out of the road.

My anxiety was worse than ever, and my working environment and schedule, well, they didn't help.

I felt like I needed to try to go to sleep, because I didn't have much time to sleep, so I needed to maximize what time I had. It felt like I was rushing to get to sleep, when apparently this is counterproductive to how sleep really works. You shouldn't have to push yourself to sleep. Your body should be able to do it naturally. Hence the phrase *fall to sleep*. You don't have to try to fall. Gravity should be doing that for you.

All of that counterproductivity led to a strange sleep phobia—at least, that's the best title I can give it. I'd love to say that it was simple insomnia, but that almost seems too general. It doesn't capture what I was living with. I've heard that mental illness takes different forms as you age, and this fear of sleep was the first time my anxiety started to overshadow my regular life. I mean, don't get me wrong, I'd get anxious and have a hard time concentrating. Sometimes it would cause me stomach problems or diarrhea. For the most part, though, I was able to function.

Or at least, I thought I was functioning.

But being afraid to fall asleep took my mental illness to a new and all-around freaky level.

And I suppose it wasn't the act of sleeping that I was afraid of. I craved sleep. I wanted it more than anything. Sleep was the cat's pajamas. I loved it! But it was the act of falling asleep that was problematic. It was in the space between being awake and falling asleep that I was afraid. It was in that short journey, when I could see sleep like it was the light at the end of a tunnel. I'd be so close, and suddenly I'd jerk awake, terrified, in the grip of a panic attack. I'd start sweating. Maybe throw up. Then I'd go back to bed and try again, only for it to happen over and over.

And the reasons for this sleep phobia are still murky to me. Part of me wants to say that it was because of all the chaos in my life and that perhaps subconsciously I didn't want to fall asleep because I might miss something, like losing Grandma. Or maybe it was just a by-product of my body trying to process everything.

Regardless, what I know for sure is that I would sometimes go days with little or no sleep, sitting up during the day with tightness in my stomach, only to go to work and be unable to eat without throwing up.

I found out that with enough sleep loss you can hallucinate, which in so many ways was both awesome and terrifying in a toy store. I had these fits of sleepless rage, and I would take them out on the toys, punching a stuffed Winnie the Pooh or the depressed but ultimately lovable Eeyore in the Hundred Acre Wood section. I once ripped Christopher Robin's head clean off for no legitimate reason. I just wanted to rip his head off, and it felt pretty good in the moment, but then I looked at this poor headless stuffed boy, and I felt terrible. I hid his head and torso behind some shelves.

That raw anger at my life, my situation, my inability to fall asleep, and the way I just wanted to punch the world in the face reminded me of my mother.

I didn't do any drugs during this time, even though I was surrounded by people using drugs all night long. But in some ways, that was a blessing because it made hiding my insomnia and hallucinations easier. I was already good at hiding my anxiety. I think most people with mental illness are the best actors, because we get up each day and put on a production of ourselves living a mental illness–free life, so it was natural for me to never tell anyone about my inability to sleep or my phobia of falling asleep.

Not Grandma.

Not my dad, for sure. We just didn't have that kind of relationship.

I was dating someone who also worked at the toy store. We'd been together for a while, and I hid my insomnia, hallucinations, and fear that I was going insane from her most passionately.

On the whole, my life became this mixture of reality and dream. I couldn't trust what I was seeing. I was never fully awake, but I never really slept.

I remember an instance when a whole wall of Tickle Me Elmos started talking and moving, but I was the only one seeing it, and I swear they were saying my name. They were asking me to play with them. But I didn't want to play with them, so I started crying a little.

I'd never felt so crazy in my whole life.

Millions was with me at the time. He asked what was wrong. I didn't say anything. I just kept staring at all those Elmos harassing me. Millions started laughing and said, "Whoa, man! I don't know what you're on, but you must be high outta ya mind!"

I didn't correct him. I just let him think that I was high on something because it seemed easier to live under those assumptions than to say out loud that I was going insane.

And to be real, it's not like this was a hard sale. Most people assumed I was using drugs. It's not that I ever admitted to it. I just didn't deny it, and that seemed to be enough.

One morning about six o'clock, at the end of my shift, after I'd gone a particularly long stretch without any real sleep, I was washing my hands in the restroom when a burly coworker came in. He'd worked there only a few days. I didn't know him all that well, but in my mind, I referred to him as the lumberjack. He was a huge hairy man with massive shoulders. He was probably in his early twenties, with a big brown beard and an affinity for flannel. He kicked one of the stall doors off its hinges. Inside, with his pants down, doing his business, was Millions.

The lumberjack started dropping f-bombs and then began beating Millions in the face as he used the toilet. I'd never experienced anything so terrifying. I had no idea why this was happening, but I assumed it was related to a drug deal. All of it felt like a mob hit of some kind. Something out of a movie. I mean, who beats a man while he's using the toilet?

It was barbaric.

I wanted nothing to do with it, so I more or less ran from the restroom without drying my hands, made it outside to my truck, and drove to visit Grandma.

But the craziest part about this moment was the next day. Millions and the lumberjack came back to work as if the attack had never happened. The stall door wasn't damaged in the restroom, and Millions didn't have any bruises on his face, even though I'd watched him take a pretty hard beating.

And I was left to wonder if this moment had actually happened or if I'd just hallucinated the whole thing.

I began to wonder if I had a tumor. Or cancer. Or maybe there was a demon inside me and I needed an exorcism. I wondered if I was going full-on, kit-and-caboodle crazy, but I didn't want to be seen as crazy—so I just tucked it all inside of myself and acted like it never happened. I suffered in complete silence. My coworkers assumed I was high on drugs, when I was simply high on my own madness.

But the part that scared me the most was that the hallucinations reminded me of the voices my dad heard coming from his attic, and all of that only solidified my fear that I'd somehow bypassed the drug addiction, divorces, and jail time and taken a shortcut right to becoming my dad.

"LET'S HOPE YOU DON'T BECOME HIM"

The last time I saw Dad was over breakfast on Thanksgiving Day 2001. I was nineteen. I arrived to find him urinating on a patch of scrub oak in an open lot between a gas station and the café we'd agreed to meet at. Night frost clung to the roofs of cars, and a blistery canyon wind whipped the steam coming out the stovepipes above the café. I sat in my small red S10 pickup, the same pickup my grandmother helped me buy when I was seventeen as a trade for my getting what she called "a decent haircut," and waited for Dad to finish. I'd completed my winter contract at the toy store, and I'd since gotten a job working close to full-time at one of those big-box hardware stores. I was a student at a local open-enrollment state college, but I hadn't attended class in weeks.

Dad jerked as he finished his business, then he zipped, strutted across the lot, and walked into the café.

By the time I entered, Dad was sitting at a booth, studying the menu. He'd made an effort to fix himself up, wearing a bulky green sweater with only a few grease stains, blue Wrangler jeans, and scuffed white sneakers. The café's aroma of coffee and bacon was overshadowed by Dad's Stetson cologne, and although his face was clean-shaven, his neck and jawline were sprinkled with black and gray whiskers.

Dad chose the café because it was within walking distance of his home. He'd recently gotten his driver's license back after losing it again for driving while intoxicated. He claimed that was all a misunderstanding over his dog getting out, that he was just trying to find her. "Cops don't give a crap about your dog," he said. But even with his license back, he didn't drive all that much, and I assumed it was because he didn't have gas money and because his record of DUIs meant insuring his truck would cost a fortune. However, choosing not to drive was a very mature move for him.

We met for breakfast because no one wanted to have him over for Thanksgiving dinner. My aunt didn't want him because he looked "like death," which I felt was a fair assessment of his general appearance but not necessarily a good reason to exclude him from Thanksgiving dinner. Grandma and I were planning to eat at my aunt's, so I couldn't take him with me. But I didn't want him to be alone on Thanksgiving, so I agreed to meet him for breakfast, and after calling around I eventually found a place for him at the Thanksgiving dinner table of his most recent ex-wife.

Dad smiled as I sat at the table, and I could see black pockmarks in his gums, cavities that used to hold teeth but now held particles of food and other grime. His skin held the moist, chalky tone of long-term drug addiction, his black hair was streaked with gray and matted with grease, his eyes were sunken deep into their sockets. The way he tilted his head back to look through his bifocals and thrust out his lower lip when he found something on the menu he approved of were familiar gestures. He still reminded me of the dad he was when I was a child. The dad who adamantly cheered me on at my baseball games. The dad who wore a tan suit every Sunday. His hands were still calloused and scarred from working with sheet metal, but they were thin and tired now, and they shook when his elbows weren't resting on the table. He was 50 years old, but if outsiders were trying to guess his age, they'd have placed him much older than that.

We ordered. Dad chose the lumberjack breakfast because it had four of everything: pancakes, toast, bacon, sausage, ham, and eggs.

"I'm sure hungry," he said.

I nodded.

But I knew he wasn't all that hungry. This was the leanest I'd ever seen him. The big meal, the bulky sweater, was to make me think he was healthy.

He and I had played this game many times before: He tried to hide how sick he really was, and I pretended to believe him. But I knew I wouldn't be able to play this game for long.

I never really could.

Dad started talking about the shed attached to the house he was renting. His plan was to start another heating and air-conditioning business by installing insulation, a forced-air heater, and a workbench in the shed. At the time, he was unemployed. I think his plans with the shed were to build something like the backyard business he had when he was married to my mother. As he spoke, he smiled, and I got the impression that those were the best days of his life.

Those were the days he longed to live again.

His glory days.

"I'm worried about you," I said, and Dad told me he was worried about himself.

"I can't get this thing off the ground without some cash."

I knew Dad would most likely ask me for money, and although I always gave it to him, I promised myself that I wouldn't.

"I'm not worried about that. I'm worried about the way you look," I said.

He sat silently for a moment, his dry tongue dragging across his cracked lips. He leaned back, crossed his thin legs under the table, and said defensively, "Worry a little more about yourself. I'm fine."

Then he reached across the table with his damaged right hand and pinched a strand of my long hair in his thumb, the rest of his fingers flat and crooked, and said, "I look just fine, thank you very much. You, however, need a haircut."

I couldn't help but smile.

Our meals arrived. We sat in silence, like we often did. We blinked and gulped, memories of guilt and remorse settling on me like rain clouds. Dad struggled to chew, his jaw clamping down with short jerks, his toothless gums mashing up a sausage link. The majority of his meal was placed in a to-go box.

I picked up the check. Then, before we left, I handed him forty dollars and told him to spend it on his new business. Dad pulled out his thin leather wallet, the same wallet he'd had as long as I could remember, the one that was now bursting at the seams with business cards and receipts. He unfolded it and slid the bills inside. He didn't say thanks. He just looked at me, stuck out his lips, and smacked me on the shoulder with an open hand.

I drove Dad south, to Lake Shore, the small farming community where I'd lived with him for a short time in that parked camper. It was a 30-minute drive. Once we hit the freeway, Dad started talking about my mother. They'd been divorced for almost ten years, and I couldn't remember the last time he'd mentioned her. He asked how she was doing and about her new husband.

"You know we don't speak all that much anymore," I said.

"That's too bad," he said. "She's a good woman. Short fuse. But a good woman."

Then he started talking about the Mormon church, and how he'd been visiting one near his home.

"Suppose you think I'm a real piece of work for

the way I left your mother," he said.

I did feel that way, but I didn't really have room to speak because I'd left her too. I shrugged, and then it was silent for a moment as we traveled along I-15, and I watched as the suburbs of Provo changed to the farmland of Springville.

"Have you talked to your bishop about Mom?" I asked.

Dad stuck out his lips and shook his head. When I asked him why not, he said, "Because I don't imagine I'd be forgiven."

Dad's ex-wife lived in a large, blue, rectangular two-story farmhouse at the end of a gravel lane. I parked near the front door, and Dad looked at the weathered baby-blue siding, the black and orange stray cats lounging in the window-sill, and the miles of harvested farmland that surrounded the home. I don't think he wanted to be there, but I don't think he wanted to be alone either. We sat for a long while, listening to the wind and smelling the manure. Dad looked me up and down for a moment and said, "You're starting to look like your old man."

He let out a hard laugh that ended with a wet raspy cough. He cupped his mouth and then wiped the mucus on his jeans.

"Let's hope you don't become him."

This was the last thing he ever said to me.

"Yeah," I said. "Let's hope."

FOOTSTEPS

When I left the toy store and got a job at the hardware store, I had a short reprieve from my anxiety, and it was absolutely glorious. I started sleeping better, and the hallucinations stopped. I felt like I was becoming sane. I mean, sure, I had some anxiety, a little depression, but on the whole, I felt like I'd had a bad spell, took an unscheduled trip to Crazy Island, but it was over now. I'd survived and—bada-bing, bada-boom—I could go back to living a regular, crazy-free life.

This stretch of sanity lasted maybe three months. Then there was this one night, when I went to a concert with some friends and had to open the hardware store the next morning. I got home around 1:00 a.m. and had to be up at 5:00 a.m. I was in a rush to get to sleep but couldn't. My sleep phobia resurfaced, nasty and sharp-toothed, with bad breath and wild eyes. And suddenly my anxiety went to a new and freaky level. That morning I dragged myself into work, a disoriented train wreck of a human, knots in my stomach, smelling like throw-up and off-brand Lucky Charms, reeking of BO from sitting up all night anxiously sweating.

It took only one bad night for me to feel like I'd fallen into the pit of despair, where some six-fingered man leaned over me and said, "I've just sucked one year of your life away? . . . How do you feel?"

And all I could do was cry.

But the strange thing was, that anxiety attack didn't last hours, or even days, like I was used to.

It lasted months.

It felt like something broke in me, and the anxiety just plowed on. It was this fire, this burning nauseous feeling in my stomach that I couldn't explain. I stopped eating, because food made me nauseous.

I stopped speaking unless I absolutely had to, because I couldn't muster the strength to communicate while fighting the anxiety. This is something people don't talk much about when it comes to a long-lasting anxiety attack. It takes a significant amount of mental effort to just put one foot in front of the other. To keep moving, to get dressed, to speak, or even think when your body is flooded with anxious feelings. Those emotions, those numbing hot waves of fear and dread, they consume every ounce of you. The fear really was all I could think about. I didn't have a choice anymore, and so doing mundane things, like speaking or eating, took longer than normal, and I only did them when I absolutely had to. Just moving through my day-to-day life was exhausting, and yet I couldn't sleep, and I couldn't think, and I felt like it would never stop, almost like whatever broke in my brain was beyond repair.

I'm convinced the customers I helped assumed I was a mute. I just silently walked them to the items they were looking for and pointed. I lost close to twenty pounds in a matter of weeks, and I started to wonder once again if I had a tumor, or cancer, or some serious physical ailment, because everything I was feeling was so overwhelming.

I went to my family doctor, which led to my being referred to a therapist, which led me to the mime. Steve was this stretched-out man with exaggerated facial expressions. He used a lot of hand and arm movements and always appeared overly surprised by what I was saying. It kind of felt like I was meeting with someone who failed out of mime school, and decided to go back to regular school for a masters in counseling. (Is there such a thing as mime school? It doesn't matter . . .)

He wasn't quite seven feet tall, but he had to be close. I was a stocky five foot seven, so to me he seemed to be at least 85 percent arms and legs. He was the kind of guy you look at for a good long time and realize he would never be comfortable as an economy passenger on an airplane, and his knees would never be fully submerged in a standard-sized bathtub. I didn't know how he bought clothing that matched his legs and waist, and I assume that whenever he entered a room, he was very aware of whether there was a ceiling fan.

During that first session, he did what was called an intake. He went through a bunch of questions about how I was feeling, my family history, and my diet. He also asked quite a few

CLINT EDWARDS

questions about my mental health management, which was, without question, nil. I didn't even know mental health management was a thing until he started asking about it, nor did I really understand why we were meeting.

I still assumed I had some sort of physical problem, not a psychological issue. Or maybe I just told myself that. Part of me, a big part, knew that I was experiencing a mental health crisis, but I didn't have the language for that sort of thing. I mean, I knew I'd struggled with anxiety, but what I was going through felt so overwhelming and much of what was happening to me was physical. I was having difficulty speaking, I was losing weight, I was throwing up, I was experiencing cold sweats, I was having trouble sleeping.

Not that WebMD was around at this time. But if it were, I assume it would have given me a range of possible diagnoses, probably ranging from a stroke to brain and body failure. I'm not sure if brain and body failure is a real ailment, but it did feel like everything was failing and I was more or less a walking corpse. If my doctor had said, "You are dead. Contact a mortician," instead of, "I'm sending you to a therapist," I would have just nodded and spent what little money I had on a nice coffin.

Steve held a clipboard, and checked off boxes, and scribbled notes here and there, his face twisting and contorting, his eyebrows moving almost independently of his face, his body motions clearly communicating one simple phrase: *I'm concentrating.*

During our second meeting, Steve diagnosed me with depression and general anxiety disorder, and I laughed at him. It was this hysterical, vein-popping-out-of-your-forehead, *Batman*'s Joker-style laughter. I hadn't laughed in months—I don't think I'd even cracked a smile. But when Steve made his diagnosis, I just couldn't contain it.

His bodily motions, the way his legs jutted out before him, his massive hands and long fingers stopping on invisible barriers, all of it looked like he was trapped in an invisible box of emotion. It was like his body was trying so hard to do the talking for his mouth. It felt like he was trying to use his mind, body, and soul to break the news easily. But the more he talked, the more I laughed, until my face was red and I was gasping for air. What I was dealing with felt so obvious, but it wasn't until he said it out loud that it all clicked: the anxiety, the self-loathing, the stomach pains, the weight loss, the sleepless nights . . .

It felt like I could finally see something that was stupidly obvious, like when you chuckle to yourself after finding that thing you turned the house upside down to find, not realizing it was in your pocket the whole time. It felt like he'd stripped away all my defense mechanisms, all my lies and denial and confusion, and put them out on the table for me to see, and I had no other option but to laugh at how nasty it all was.

Looking back at this moment, I'm kind of surprised he didn't recommend I move into a psychiatric hospital.

During one of our meetings, Steve told me that I should begin exercising because it would help me relax at night and stave off my anxiety. I don't want to say I was a lazy person. Or at least I didn't identify myself as one. But I will say this: In high school, when we were told to run a mile, I was that kid who leisurely walked along the track with a bag of Cheetos in one hand and a bottle of Coke in the other, my classmates passing me as I struggled to lick the orange dust from my fingers.

But I was so anxious and depressed that I followed Steve's recommendations with this heretofore unseen voraciousness. I figured if I just did what he said, I could make the internal pain go away. And yes, what I was feeling was painful—the tightness in my stomach, the hot waves of anxiety, the exhaustion, the confusion, the tense muscles along my neck, and the almost endless headaches from trying so hard to just function.

So when Steve casually said, "You should start exercising more," I started riding my bike each day, and it helped. When my body was in motion, I wasn't so anxious. And not feeling so anxious after feeling mind-numbingly anxious for two months felt amazing. Riding five miles a day led to ten miles a day. Then twenty. Then forty.

Working out each day helped at first. I didn't feel as anxious when I was exercising. But then it became something more. Instead of believing that exercise might help reduce my anxiety, I started to believe that not exercising would cause me anxiety.

Exercise became the prescription I had to take.

I blinked, and I was living in a repetitive hell of exercising four to eight hours a day, never missing a single day, all of it feeling like I was trying to outrun my anxiety.

Yet somehow, I never achieved abs.

Steve suggested that I try meditating and keeping a regular bedtime schedule, and suddenly it became gospel.

It became the law I lived by.

I followed a rigorous, unstopping, invariable, "This is my contract and it cannot be changed" routine. I went to bed at the exact same time and woke up at the exact same time. Ten or twenty minutes of variation, and I went into a rambling anxious fit.

Sure, this didn't happen overnight. It happened over a span of weeks. But eventually, I had a schedule of exercise and meditation, and it could not be broken under any circumstances.

I had to meditate at exactly the right hour. Steve said I should stop drinking caffeine, so I cut it out of my life like it was a hate crime. He suggested I change my diet and eat healthier meals because a healthy body wouldn't be so anxious, and within a week, eating the right foods, at the right time, became my contract. Anything that diverted me from my exercise and diet and sleep schedule would push me over the edge into absolute, unwavering, mad-eyed panic.

Everything—every movement, every thought, every action—became about avoiding the next panic attack. My anxiety told me that if I didn't follow my schedule, if I didn't get my workouts in, I wouldn't get to sleep, and if I didn't get to sleep, I'd have a panic attack. And slowly the thought of having anxiety made me anxious, and slowly, not engaging in anxiety-avoiding activities became a source of anxiety.

My life, my schedule, my routine was set in stone, rigid and unchangeable. Avoiding anxiety was at the front of my mind, on the tip of my tongue. It was the devil and the angel on my shoulders.

It was my prison guard.

It was the voice I heard at all hours, 24-7.

None of it made sense to anyone but me, and yet somehow people really admired my commitment to exercise and diet. My coworkers complimented me on my good health and asked me how I did it. They asked for advice on healthy living.

They looked at me with complete envy.

"You really are getting yourself together," they'd say. "You are an inspiration."

I accepted their compliments, I admit. Friends would ask where I found the motivation to do vigorous cycling for four to six hours a day, and I'd tell them casually that "I sometimes get anxious when I don't exercise or eat right," never going too deep into the facts of my anxiety disorder.

They'd respond with, "I wish I had that problem," followed by a chuckle, almost like they longed for a tapeworm or malaria because it might help them finally drop that spare tire.

But the reality was, my anxiety had flamed on and, according to my therapist, had become full-blown obsessive-compulsive disorder. And let me be clear: This was not the kind of OCD that people jokingly talk about when organizing their DVD collection or loading their dishwasher, or any other instance they use OCD to explain their flaming bull crap obsessions that in reality are just preferences. In fact, I hate when people use the term *OCD* in those ways, because they have no idea what it's like really living with it.

Obsessive-compulsive disorder completely consumed my life.

But when Steve made that diagnosis, I didn't laugh—which was funny, considering the only connection I had to obsessive-compulsive disorder was from the comedy *What About Bob?* This was a movie I found hilarious before I was diagnosed with obsessive-compulsive disorder. Who doesn't enjoy watching Bill Murray drive his vacationing therapist crazy with his tics, and questions, and inability to stop following his therapist around? And sure, Bob had a longer list of mental health concerns than just obsessive-compulsive disorder. But the moment a therapist sat across from me and said, "You are showing signs of obsessive-compulsive disorder," all I could do was wonder if I was now Bob.

There were characters in movies I wanted to be. I wanted to look like a shirtless Brad Pitt in *Fight Club*. That was pretty high on the list. I wanted to be as naturally brilliant as Matt Damon in *Good Will Hunting*. And I secretly wanted to be Gandalf in *The Lord of the Rings*, because dang, how cool would that be? I mean, who wouldn't feel satisfied with their life as a full-fledged wizard? Maybe I could even cast a spell and get rid of this whole anxiety thing while also casting another spell that gave me Brad Pitt's abs?

But never did I want to be as crazy as Bob, and it was in that moment that I realized I could never tell anyone—not one single soul—about this diagnosis.

In terms of exercise and diet, this was the healthiest I'd ever lived, and yet my mental health was a total train wreck. There was this voice telling me to go, go, go—all of it to avoid a panic attack. I'd never been more depressed. Thoughts of suicide were my backdrop, my foundation, my hiding spot, my breakfast, lunch, and dinner. They were always there, like that friend that doesn't encourage you to get help but instead says, "Yup, you're right. You do suck. Might as well kill yourself" in a half-serious, half-joking tone—yet you can't seem to cut that person out of your life.

I lived in Utah, so I took up cross-country mountain biking. I'd ride every day. When the temperature soared past 100 degrees in July and August, I was out there, in the desert sun, riding. For rainy days, I had an indoor bike. And whenever I had a panic attack in the night, I believed, in my heart and soul, that it was because I didn't exercise enough, so I'd exercise more the next several days.

I took up running. I took up weight lifting and yoga. I worked days in the garden center at the hardware store and spent most of that time hauling paver stones, retaining-wall blocks, bags of topsoil, and heavy potted shrubs for customers, all of it in the hot sun. Between moving heavy things, I did push-ups or pull-ups on the bars that were used to hang potted plants.

I was obsessed, but not with losing weight, or getting stronger, or staying healthy, like so many normal people who turn to exercise. I was determined to make myself too tired to be anxious and to make sure that when I went to bed I was absolutely exhausted. And yet I couldn't seem to out-exercise my anxiety, regardless of how hard I pushed my body.

I exercised so much I sometimes urinated blood, and yet I was terrified to stop, and each time I had a panic attack, I turned the exercise up a notch. One afternoon, I wrecked on my mountain bike and was knocked out cold. I don't know how long I was unconscious. I went to the hospital and had a CT scan. The doctor told me I had a pretty bad concussion and a mild brain hemorrhage and I needed to take it easy for several weeks. "Don't exercise and avoid bright lights. Try not to think too much," he said. Then he told me I needed to come back for a follow-up appointment.

The moment he said, "Don't exercise," I was hit with a wave of terror. I never went back to that doctor. I was given a printout with all of his recommendations, and I threw it in the trash outside the hospital. I went home and rode my stationary bike, because my workout had been cut short after I'd been knocked out and I was afraid I wouldn't sleep.

I was attending an open-enrollment college just like I told people I would. I had two classes, Introduction to American History and Student Success. I attended the history class twice and the student success class four times. I was leaving Student Success on the morning of September 11, 2001. There was a crowd of students gathered around a TV in one of the hallways, watching smoke roll out of the World Trade Center. I watched as the first building collapsed. Students covered their mouths with their hands. People were pale. Frightened. Shocked. I looked at the TV just long enough to comprehend what was happening. I stood there in shock for no more than ten minutes before my anxiety kicked in, before my right hand started to shake.

Everyone around me talked about war. They talked about the tragedy of it all, and they wondered if there would be more attacks on the United States. They worried about the people in the towers. The newscasters were horrified. One of the greatest American tragedies was right there, happening in front of me. It was horrible to watch, and there was a logical part of me that recognized that fact. I knew that I should make what was happening in New York my priority, and yet . . . I couldn't.

All I could think was, *Get to your workout so you won't have anxiety.*

I left the school and drove straight to the bike trail.

Along with a therapist, I also met with a psychiatrist during this time, and he prescribed numerous medications, some to take daily and some to take occasionally. I was meeting with two different family doctors, and they gave me other prescriptions. My therapist recommended herbal supplements. I took Celexa for depression, Xanax for anxiety, Ambien and Sonata for sleep. I took Klonopin and can't even remember why. I took a long list of supplements: melatonin, St. John's wort, zinc, B vitamins, rhodiola, omega-3, to name a few. I can't even remember what each of them did.

The best pills were the ones I was supposed to take occasionally: Xanax and Ambien. They were my all-time favorites because they made me feel numb inside. It felt like they turned my brain off, and when I wasn't thinking so much about avoiding my anxiety, I could laugh again. I could wander about aimlessly and get so comfortable on the sofa I wet my pants a little.

But what was best about Ambien was that it made me forget. It's a sleeping pill, and I can't understate how amazing it was for me. Sometimes I'd take it during the day, and I'd lose long stretches of time. I felt checked out, like the anxiety I was fighting was simply cut out of my life with scissors, and in the blackness of amnesia, the fear was gone—and, well, when you've been feeling anxiety, dread, depression for days on end, the blackness of sleeping pills feels as wonderful as a tropical vacation.

I knew my dad would go from one doctor to another to get pain prescriptions, treating clinics like drug dealers, and although my early anxiety, particularly in high school, was rooted in a fear of becoming my father, I couldn't believe how easily I'd started to fall directly into his footsteps. I'd taken very few prescriptions before my OCD.

But everything was different now. Each morning and evening, I gazed at my handful of pills, feeling like they were a loaded gun, wondering if I was becoming an addict. Yet my anxiety, my depression shoved me into a spiral of medications and exercise that I couldn't get out of. I never told any of these doctors about the others, and they never asked if I was seeing anyone else.

I don't really know how many doctors my dad was seeing. He kept that information close to his chest. I was pretty sure that what I was up to wasn't nearly at the scale of my dad's doctor shopping to get medications, but it was far closer to mimicking him than I'd ever been before.

The detail that gave me the most pause was that one of those family doctors I mentioned earlier was the same doctor I'd met with as a child. He delivered me when I was born. I knew him incredibly well, and I trusted him, and I honestly believed he was a good man with good intentions. I still do, actually. But he was also the same doctor that did those first surgeries on my dad, the ones that went wrong, and he was the same doctor that most likely began prescribing him opioids. He was also the first doctor to prescribe me Xanax and Ambien, and knowing all of this felt like a full-circle moment. It felt like I'd finally found the beginning of my father's path, and I was now on it.

And yet I was afraid to stop. I think that was one of the hardest parts of my mental illness at this time. Going to doctors was a source of anxiety because it reminded me of my dad, and yet not going to doctors was a source of anxiety because I so desperately wanted the medication to keep myself from having anxiety. When I think about that reality, there is a lot of irony in having anxiety about the doctors who are treating you for anxiety, but at the time, I wasn't in the mood for irony, so instead I threw up and then went for a bike ride.

I dropped out of college during my first semester. Or maybe I didn't drop out. I assume dropping out is an actual process in which you withdraw from classes. Perhaps make a proclamation to the school. Perhaps send an email. I don't really know.

I just stopped going.

With all that exercise, I didn't have time for school. I was living with my girlfriend at the time, but the relationship was falling apart. I didn't have enough emotions available to be a good boyfriend, or even much of a friend, and slowly we became closer to roommates than a couple. I was empty, having nothing left to give the relationship. All of it made me think about my mother, back when she was working those long hours and had nothing left emotionally to give me as a child, and I realized that I was also following in her footsteps.

Yes, I was having regular meetings with a therapist, but I never told him about my fear of becoming my parents. I never told any of the doctors I was meeting with about that fear either. I was afraid to talk to anyone about it, really. Opening up would only confirm that it was true. I was afraid that if I told any doctor about my father's drug addiction and my mother's depression, they would just nod and say, "Yes, you are becoming them. It's clearly in your DNA." And the thought of having a doctor confirm that fear felt like a surefire way to send my mental illness to a dangerous level. I didn't know what would push me from suicidal thoughts to actions. But having a doctor confirm my deepest, darkest fear—that I was becoming my parents—felt like a definite way to do it. So I never said anything, as a way to keep that fear under control.

So much of what I did during this time was about trying desperately to gain control over my anxiety and depression, but what I was really doing was losing all control of my life. I wasn't my parents. I knew that, and yet I couldn't help but feel like I was strapped in a roller coaster. Someone pulled the lever and I was heading up the track, destined to follow my parents' examples.

One month after I saw my dad on Thanksgiving Day 2001, a police officer visited me at work. He was young, probably in his mid-twenties, in full uniform, with dark-framed glasses. We stood in front of the hardware store, and he told me Dad had died, alone, in his bedroom.

"We don't know how long he'd been dead," he said. "We're still figuring out the cause as well, but we don't suspect foul play or anything. It was most likely natural causes." Then he told me that a neighbor called it in, but I can't remember what that neighbor noticed exactly. Maybe it was a smell, or perhaps it was a lack of activity. I hadn't been visiting Dad much because my workouts didn't allow the time. I didn't have time for much of anything except working enough hours to pay for food, rent, and medical bills.

But one of the real reasons I'd stopped visiting Dad was because his skinny frame, his missing teeth, all of it felt like a glimpse into my future. Every time I thought about him in relation to the doctors I was seeing and the medications I was taking, I couldn't help but make a connection, and I struggled with that now more than at any other time.

Telling Grandma that her youngest son had died must have been the hardest part. She was still living with my aunt. It was evening and dark outside, and Grandma was in red and blue flannel pajamas. I sat next to her on my aunt's sofa, and I can't remember exactly what I said, but I remember feeling it was a blunt, simple, and sudden explanation. Something as simple as "Dad died." I didn't know how to make it easier, so I just said it simply and quickly.

She let out this very long wail at first, and then eased into a long, hard sob. She reached out for me with her good hand and then buried her face in my shoulder. She cried and shook as I held her. But then she took a breath and sat up straight. She gripped my knee with her hand and said, "I suppose we knew it was coming, didn't we?"

It was one of those moments when time moved both quickly and slowly. She held me for what seemed like forever, but once she let go, I wished she hadn't. Yes, I'd known my father was going to die. I'd known that for a long time. But it wasn't in the "everyone dies" way. As I looked back on the ten years between when he left my mother and when he died, it was clear that this day wasn't far off. As I thought about his life, I struggled to feel sorrow over his passing. It was a strange realization. I should have been heartbroken. He was my father. But instead I was a mixture of emotions: anxiety, uncertainty, loss. But the most potent feeling was one of relief. I felt like something I'd dreaded was now over, and I felt guilty for feeling that way. For feeling relieved knowing that I not only didn't have to worry about my father eventually dying from his addictions but also that I didn't have to worry about his decisions and his actions and how they might negatively affect my life anymore.

A few days after Dad's death, I helped clean his apartment. I entered through the small shop on the side of his rental house. It wasn't much, probably the size of a cozy bedroom, but it had a workbench, and tools, and welders off to the side. It smelled like metal shavings, and it had some sheet metal along the wall, and I could feel that optimism he had about starting another business the last time we spoke.

The smell of his passing still lingered the day my brother, half-brother, and I came to collect his things. It was a heavy mixture of urine, body odor, and something I couldn't quite identify but assumed was decay. We opened all the windows and doors to air out the small, one-bedroom apartment he was renting in American Fork, Utah. In the living room, a thrift-store leather footstool sat next to a bright green floral-print glider, and a naked light bulb hung from the ceiling along with three dangling spiral strips of flypaper that were so thick with flies I couldn't see the sticky yellow surface underneath. There were no photos or paintings. The walls were as white as the day Dad moved in.

As we walked through his apartment, I thought about what Grandma told me the day I told her about Dad's death. We had known this was coming, and in that moment, I felt relief. But now, being in his apartment, experiencing it . . . Well, I don't know if there is any way to fully anticipate the numbness of losing your father. His old mattress on the floor, the carpet along the hallway, the wall next to the restroom, were all a mess of body fluid. I know that some people pay for cleaners in a situation like this, but my brothers and I, we just handled it, and in a lot of ways I wish we hadn't. It was so easy to see his final moments stained inside that house.

All of it—the body fluid, how skinny he was before he died, his missing teeth, the years of drug addiction—made it seem obvious to me that he died from a drug overdose, but I don't ever remember being told an official cause of death.

But what was so odd was that as I went through his wallet, I found a Mormon temple recommend that had been issued in April of that year. In Mormonism, having an active temple recommend is the golden standard for members. It means that you are following the values of the church and you are worthy to enter the temple, which to us is basically like walking right on into God's own house. And in God's house, you can't have mud on your shoes, and you must have cleaned behind your ears, and you must have brushed your teeth. Nothing unclean can enter the Lord's house. For Mormons, a temple recommend is a big deal, so to say that I was shocked to find a recommend in his wallet is an understatement.

I stood there and looked at it for some time. To get this wallet-sized document, Dad must have sat across from church leaders and said he was following the Word of Wisdom. That's the doctrine that spells out that Mormons are to abstain from drugs and alcohol. But the doctrine doesn't say anything about prescription painkillers, and at the time, I felt certain he must have lied to get that recommend.

Days after cleaning out his apartment, I stood in the mortuary, wearing his old leather belt with his name printed on the back. Dad wore that belt nearly every day of his life. I listened to the sentiments "I'm sorry your dad turned out this way" and "He used to be a good man."

By this point in his life, I hadn't ever met someone who had anything good to say about Dad, so to hear people say, "He used to be a good man" just felt like a platitude. I didn't believe a word of it, even though I honestly wanted to. I wanted to believe that there was something redeemable about this man who was my father, because if I could find something of quality in him, maybe I might not be so afraid of ending up exactly like him, 50 years old, toothless, and dead from a drug overdose—a future that felt more and more possible as I considered the way I was beginning to abuse my own medications.

I was sad that day. Not because I lost my father, but because now he'd never get the chance to turn his life around and become the father I always longed for.

Months after his funeral, I started having nightmares. Or maybe it was a vision. It's hard to tell with something like that. I watched him die through his eyes, and it felt like I was dying. Sometimes I was him, dying alone, on the mattress on the floor. Sometimes I was just standing in the room, watching it happen, not able to move my head to look away or close my eyes.

It was more frightening than any of my panic attacks, and I know this all sounds crazy, but hey, this is a book about my crazy, so stick with me here. If you are not the kind of person who believes in life after death and ghosts trying to influence the living, I understand how this might appear to you. But regardless of your ideology or your feelings about life after death, at the time, I kinda felt like my dad was warning me. Like he was trying to send me a message from beyond the grave (insert scary ghost sounds).

Or maybe it was just my subconscious trying to process a difficult event.

I don't really know what was going on, but what I can say is that I kept having this dream, sometimes every night for a week, sometimes only once a month. It went on like that for almost two years. It was the nightmares that changed me. Somehow that same horrible, dreadful dream hitting me night after night, like I was watching the same horrific film from different angles, gave me the strength to regain my life.

One morning I woke up and I knew, in my heart, my head, my soul, that I had to be something different or I was going to end up exactly like my dad.

In the winter of 2002, I threw away the bulk of my medications because they reminded me of my father. I stopped meeting with my therapist, and my psychiatrist, and the family practitioners I'd been getting medications from because they were doctors, and doctors reminded me of my father. I stopped exercising for hours on end and went back to church. I looked at my father's life, and at a dead sprint, I ran as far away from it as I could. It was anxiety that pushed me into living a life consumed by obsessive-compulsive disorder, and it was the deep fear that I was going to die like my father that pulled me out of it.

PART 3

LIVING WITH DENIAL

Tick, Tick, Tock

As I unpacked my things, Mom stepped from the hallway and into the room where I'd be staying, looked me in the eyes, and told me not to touch the 48-inch Roman-numeral clock or the hardwood picture frames. She listed a number of things that I wasn't to touch, and I wondered how I was going to live with her without touching anything. It felt like I'd moved into a museum, and Mom was the museum director, and all eyes were on me because I was obviously an untrustworthy, suspicious-looking character.

A few years ago, I read a story about some dude that wanted to get an amazing selfie next to a priceless sculpture. He leaned on the thing, took a photo, and then ended up breaking off three of the sculpture's toes. It was a pretty ridiculous situation, and today I realize my mother assumed I was going to be the selfie guy. At any moment, I would break some rule, and I'd break her things, and she'd be left to cry something that I had heard far too often as a child: "I knew this was a bad idea!"

A phrase that I often interpreted in my youth as "I knew *you* were a bad idea."

She pointed at the top drawers of the dresser, then the closet, and told me I could put my clothing in those two places and nowhere else. She was in her late forties, her hair still bleached blond, same as it was when I left her Provo home at fourteen, but it was cut shorter now. Her house was in Cedar Hills, a small suburb in Utah County, set snugly against the mountains. When I was growing up, it was mostly apple orchards, but those were gone now and it was predominantly middle-class housing. Her new husband was a retired power line worker she'd met at her job collecting payments for the power company. They'd been married for several years, and as far as I could tell, most of the financial burden that caused her to work endless hours when I was a child was behind her. Sure, she still worked that same job at the power company, but that was it.

She had a few more wrinkles than I'd remembered, but her voice held the same old authority. Although she was an inch or two shorter than me now, I still felt like I was looking up at her as she spoke, pointing at the things I was not to touch, her right index finger jabbing exactly like it did when I was child.

I couldn't help but feel frightened.

Or maybe a better word would be *intimidated*.

I mean, I was technically an adult. Right? I was 21. I could vote, and drink if I wanted, and drive a car, and take out a loan if a bank would have me. Which they wouldn't. Believe me, I tried. Regardless of my poor financial situation, I was indeed an adult, and yet my mom still totally, completely, without question intimidated the crap out of me, and I couldn't help but sense that anxiety I felt as a child creep up through my chest and into my neck as she spoke. My right hand started to shake, and I really wondered if this was going to work—and yet I didn't have a lot of options.

She looked at my clothing, which was piled in a heap on the bed—my stained, stretched-out, and depressed socks, faded shirts, and worn-out boxer shorts spackled with holes—and told me they should be thrown out. When I unpacked at my mom's, I pulled my clothing out of garbage sacks because that's what I'd put them in when I moved from my apartment, and while I didn't think about it at the time, garbage sacks were exactly what I'd used when I left my mom's house the first time.

"Clothing like that makes you look homeless," Mom said. "Are you homeless?" Then she paused for a moment, and whispered to herself, "Of course you are. You had to move in with your mother."

I didn't necessarily like thinking of myself in those terms, but in reality, I was 21 and flat effing broke. The girl I was living with tried to leave me for a mutual friend, so we broke up. Not that I'm trying to justify cheating behavior or anything, but I couldn't really blame her. Well, actually, at the time I totally blamed her. I was flaming pissed about it when I found out.

I was hurt.

I had emotions.

But looking back now, I was as emotionally

available as a finicky house cat, only interested in giving her attention when I had time between workouts, which wasn't often. I think the only reason she stayed with me as long as she did was because my father died, and she felt bad dumping me after something like that, which to her credit was very kind. But it wasn't a healthy reason to stay in a relationship.

I couldn't afford to pay the rent on my own. I was in debt from buying exercise equipment, purchasing high-end mountain bikes and gear, going to doctor visits, and putting tacos on my credit card. And listen to me, it was a shocking number of tacos.

I am not proud of this.

Dad was dead. Grandma was in a care facility, and my aunt told me I couldn't move back into Grandma's house, even though no one was living there. She just didn't trust me to take care of the house alone, which really wasn't a bad assessment, considering I was a pretty massive slob at the time. But I was angry about it, because I had only one other option and it was . . . well . . . to move in with my mother. And let me be clear, I was as shocked as the residents of London on Christmas morning when Ebenezer Scrooge started singing carols the moment my mother said, "Yes, I have a room you can stay in."

But the tone of her voice, the way she said flatly, "It's fine," made me wonder if she'd been waiting for this day for a long time. But I wasn't sure if it was because she knew I'd come crawling back or if it was because she hoped that maybe, just maybe, my moving back in with her might repair our many years of hardly speaking.

Maybe it was a little of both.

But you know, a lot of children who have to move back in with their mother in their twenties often feel pretty bad about it because it's kind of a "failure to launch" sort of moment. It makes you feel like you tried to spread your wings and make a go at this world but flew too close to the sun by buying too many tacos, so you crashed and burned, and now all of your extended family gets to quote lines from the movie *Step Brothers* when you're not around. Not that *Step Brothers* had come out yet. I moved back in with my mother in 2002, but you get the idea.

I totally felt all those "Ugh, I have to move back in with my mother," failure-at-life emotions. Sure. But it was a little more complicated considering I hadn't lived with Mom since I was fourteen, and I didn't leave all that graciously. I felt bad about the way I left, but I knew I couldn't stay in her home with the way things were without hurting myself. I didn't know how to tell her about all of that. And she didn't know how to ask or to tell me that she still felt a lot of resentment for the way I left. So our solution for years was to kind of avoid each other, which seems like a petty, unadult way to handle things, but hey, that's family.

When we did talk, it was surface level, with occasional grunts and yeses and nos. There were a lot of side-eye glances and moments when we looked at each other and felt like we should say something, perhaps air it all out, but just couldn't muster the words. So the hurt and the raw feelings of resentment just sat in our guts, and festered, and got worse, never better, over time—never to the point where we could speak casually or even remotely comfortably.

But now I was living in her home again, and we kind of had to talk, and it felt like all those years of not talking and all that baggage of hurt feelings was just hanging over our heads.

"I'm just trying to get my life back together." I said.

"Okay," she said. "Okay. I don't understand you, but I'm willing to help you."

Then she placed one hand on my lower spine, the other on my chest, and pushed me vertical, forcing my thumbs from my sagging jeans. "Stand up straight," she said. "You're developing a hump." Then she stepped back, her arms tense, index finger pointing with each word. "I don't want you to think that I don't love you. You're my son. But I want you to know that I don't necessarily like you here."

For weeks, our exchanges were exactly like that one, so we avoided each other as much as possible, which really was on-brand for us. I knew when she got up for work, so I'd wait until I heard her car pull out, even if it meant I arrived at work late. I did the same thing when I got home, waiting around the corner until I saw her pull in and go inside, and then I'd give her time to go downstairs.

I think she did something similar with me, because I could hear her go downstairs each time I left my bedroom.

But the intolerable part was not how we avoided each other, or the way she sometimes just stared at me from another room, eyeing me up and down like I was a full garbage can ready to be taken out. For me, it was living in a room with that stupid 48-inch clock.

My anxiety over sleep caused me to develop a clock phobia. I Googled it once, and it's called chronomentrophobia. You can use that next time you play Scrabble, and everyone will say it's not real, and then *boom*! It will be real, and you can send me gifts.

You're welcome.

Please realize a couple of things. This here is a self-diagnosis. No therapist ever pulled his glasses down, looked me in the eyes, and said with a Freudian accent, "You suffer from chrono-mentrophobia, and that's just weird, so don't tell anyone about it because no one will believe you—but it might come in handy next time you play Scrabble."

I wasn't exactly afraid of clocks during the day. Just as it got closer to nighttime. Usually after 7:00 p.m. Clocks seemed to say, "You need to get ready to go to bed," or, "Night is coming." As each second passed, each minute, each ticktock, I was reminded that nighttime was drawing closer, and nighttime meant anxiety, and seeing a clock in the evening kind of made me freak the eff out.

Now realize that it wasn't like when you show a vampire a cross. I didn't smash clocks, or light them on fire, or put my hands over my face and let out a hissing sound. They didn't make my skin melt, although in some ways that might have been handy. If I ran into a clock and it made my skin melt, it would have legitimized my fear of clocks. But unfortunately, mental illness doesn't work that way. The skin melting is all in your mind and, well, that tends to delegitimize your struggle to outsiders—particularly your mother, so I didn't mention any of this to her.

I didn't tell anyone about it, actually, because it made me feel like a freaking weirdo.

Anyway, clocks sent me into a panic, and that Roman-numeral behemoth in my room, the one I wasn't allowed to touch, made me feel like I was living inside Big-effing-Ben.

I was doing much better with the OCD. And yet this clock in my bedroom was about to send me to a psychiatric hospital. I needed it out of my room, so one evening, as Mom was downstairs, I decided to just pull it off the wall and put it up in the other bedroom all sneaky-like and hope she didn't notice, something that I thought would be simple considering we'd been going out of our way to avoid each other.

I'd just gotten it off the wall, all ninja-ish, and almost like she had an alarm on the thing, I heard Mom rushing upstairs. She sprang into my room as I had the monster clock in a bear hug. I was caught red-handed touching something she'd asked me specifically not to touch, and I could feel the anger swelling inside of her. I watched it burn from her chest and into her face, and suddenly I was thirteen years old again and completely terrified of her. These were the moments when I'd hide from her in my closet as a child, and I couldn't believe that fear was still so present.

In the Avengers movie series, there are words in Russian that activate the Winter Soldier, this Soviet-brainwashed super soldier that's like 100 years old with a vibranium arm. When they are said, he can't help but fall under their spell and turn into a killing machine. His big struggle is getting that Russian programming out of his brain so he can go back to being a nice guy from Brooklyn who doesn't engage in espionage, murder, and acrobatics. And the reason I bring this up is because as I experienced my mother's anger, I felt like I had some old programming in my brain. No, I didn't turn into a super soldier killing machine like the Winter Soldier. Although there is a part of me that wishes that would've happened, because then, you know, I'd be an Avenger instead of just mentally ill, and frankly that sounds more satisfying.

Instead, at the age of 21, I turned into a scared little boy, the same as I was before I left my mother's house to live with my grandmother, and suddenly I couldn't speak.

I couldn't move.

I was a deer in headlights.

"I knew this was a mistake. I just knew!" she exclaimed.

Mom accused me of trying to steal the clock, which I found offensive considering stealing a massive Roman-numeral clock would be like stealing a red-hot poker I planned to stick inside my anus.

But I wasn't sure how to explain all of that, so I took a breath, my hands still on the clock, and turned my back to my mother.

I didn't look her in the face.

I was afraid to.

"I'm not stealing it. I just wanted to move it to another room," I said. I thought what I said sounded reasonable. Logical. Rational.

A very simple request.

But she didn't see it that way. She in turn found it offensive, mentioning that she "bought that clock for that room alone, and that's exactly where it needs to be."

It was quiet for a moment. I put the clock back on the wall, and turned around to see her standing in the doorway in black sweatpants and an old T-shirt. She took a breath once I stopped touching the clock and asked me why I wanted it out. At first I refused to tell her because I knew my reasoning was crazy, so I just told her it was ugly, which she saw as a personal attack.

"It's a very nice clock," she said. "I paid a lot of money for it. What would you even know about nice things?" She gestured at my baggy jeans with holes in the knees and skate shoes that had gray tape along the bottom to patch holes.

We argued some more, and then she finally said something that gave me pause.

"I like things where they need to be, and if they are moved it makes me . . ." She paused and shook for a moment, and finally said, "Anxious."

Her hand began to shake, same as mine did. Her wide eyes, her tense shoulders, the way she tilted her head to the side because her neck was getting stiff with anxiety, all of it was so familiar. And sure, in this moment, I felt like the scared little boy who had left home after dark so many years ago, but I was looking at her through a different lens now, and it was almost like I could see the steam of our shared mental illness rising off her.

And suddenly the organization of her house, the way she felt such relief when burning my father's backyard messes, the rage that was the backdrop of my childhood fell into place, and I realized her life was about keeping things organized. Much like how nighttime, sleep, exercise, and clocks triggered my anxiety, disorganization triggered hers. Of course she struggled raising children, because they are mess makers. And yes, she couldn't handle my father, because he was unpredictable, unorganized, and secretive.

All she had to do was say the word *anxious*, and I realized for the first time that my mother must suffer from a mental illness very similar to mine. And true to her form, she didn't say much about her struggles. She still kept to her code of silence when it came to this sort of thing. But for me, a boy raised by a woman who was so clearly struggling with mental illness and yet never spoke openly about it, this single moment of shared connection hit me in the heart with a wave of empathy.

It was overwhelming.

Yes, I had a hard time living with her as a child. Yes, I was afraid of her. But many of her actions, her sorrow, her fits of anger, and her suicidal thoughts during my childhood were a reaction to being placed in a very difficult situation after my father left. All of it must have exacerbated her mental illness, because before that hardship, I can't help but look back on our relationship with fondness. I think of the way she would hold me, and kiss my forehead, and care for me.

In that moment, I realized that if I'd found myself in her shoes, trying to care for a family alone, with a drug-addicted ex-husband working in the backyard, not paying child support, and brandishing his new girlfriend in view six days a week—all of it happening during a time when mental illness was terribly misunderstood and widely shunned—well, I'm not sure how I would have reacted either. I don't know how much long-term damage it would have done to me, but one thing is for sure: I'd have been very pissed off at the world.

Yes, I was still frightened of her, even then, in my twenties. To be real, even now, as I write this sentence at 38 years old, she still makes me a little nervous. But that moment of shared connection weighted me with a deeper understanding that this anxious part of her was inside of me, and that realization helped me find a way to not only feel closer to her but also forgive her and feel comfortable confiding in her.

I told her about my fear of time, and clocks, and sleep. And instead of judging me, she just stood there, and thought, and said something I think I'd always longed for her to say, "I understand."

Then she thought again for a moment and said, "I get the same way when . . ." She trembled slightly and said, "Things are out of order." She finished her sentence with a forced smile.

This was the most my mother had ever admitted to me about her mental illness, and to this day it is still the most she has ever revealed to me, but in this moment, it was enough.

We bonded that night just enough to make living together bearable. Then together we came up with a compromise that only two crazy people could birth. The clock would stay, but I could cover it with a garbage sack.

Over the next few months, we started to speak casually for the first time in years. We started to talk about our work, family, and shared friends. We had meals together. We even laughed. Every once in a while, I'd find new clothes in my room. Shirts, socks, underwear, the things I couldn't afford at the time. Then I'd check my dresser to discover that my old clothing, the ones with holes and stains, were slowly being thrown out. Her frankness was still there, because that's who she is. But the new clothing, the meals, all of it was characteristic of her. She wasn't necessarily a nurturing person, but she was a dedicated person.

The kind of mother that showed her love through service and thoughtful gifts. The kind of mother that would work as much as she needed to, even if it meant two or three jobs, to provide for her children.

I tried to return that love in a way she might understand, by doing things around the house to help out. One Saturday morning, as I was heading out to work and just after she'd made us both pancakes, she stopped me at the door and wrapped me in her arms. She gave me the warmest hug, and I couldn't remember the last time we shared an embrace like that. It must have been years. She just held me for some time, and just as those old feelings of anxiety hit me when she caught me moving the clock, the old feelings of love, and warmth, and security of being in my mother's arms—the ones that I felt before Dad left— came flooding back.

"I love you," she said.

"I love you too," I replied.

And once we were done, and I was in my truck, the motor running, I realized I was near tears, and I sat there for a moment and reflected on the goodness of that exchange.

But what I knew I had to do, well, it took me a few more months.

It was the last day of the skiing season, and Mom and I went to Sundance Mountain Resort on her invitation. The lift runs along the northeast slope of Mount Timpanogos. To our right was the mountain peak, still weighted with spring snow, runoff flowing between the rocks. To our left was a rugged view of the Wasatch Mountain Range. We were on the main lift, moving toward the ridge crest. Mom wore a black ski suit, and I wore green ski pants and a gray jacket. She commented on my mismatched winter clothes, and I told her they were on sale.

We didn't speak for a while. Bearclaw Cabin at the end of the lift was within sight. I looked at Mom, black goggles covering most of her face, and told her I was sorry.

"For what?" she asked.

"For leaving the way I did," I said.

And although I couldn't see most of her face, I could tell by the way her lower lip twisted that she knew I meant the night I moved out. In the past, we'd always talked around this subject. Never had I addressed it head-on.

"When I left, I left because I had to," I said. I told her that I never intended to hurt her. I told her I was afraid I was going to hurt myself. I asked if she could forgive me.

Before that day, I cannot recall ever telling Mom I was sorry. Not after I was sent to "truancy education" for cutting class, or for going so many years without calling her, or for all the times I forgot her birthday. And when I read that list of all the ways I was unapologetic, I see a clear correlation between me and my father. But I was trying to be different now. I wasn't working out as much. Only a couple hours a day. I wasn't abusing doctors. I wasn't taking medication outside of an occasional sleeping pill when I had nighttime anxiety. My OCD was, for the most part, in check. I'd started attending church again. I was trying to be someone different, someone other than my dad, and in doing so, it felt like the right thing to do was start apologizing.

She tapped my leg, and nodded, and it seemed clear that my apology was accepted.

We exited the lift, and as I strapped my boot into the binding I looked up to see Mom lift her goggles and rub tears from her eyes.

"YOU CAN GO . . ."

Melodie was 21. She was petite, five foot two, with short brown hair, slender hands, and slender hips, and this smile that, regardless of the moment—the stress of work, the frustration of her life, a crappy customer, whatever—was always there.

It was her bright optimism that drew me to her. I'd never met someone that seemed so happy. I'd met a lot of angry people in my life, sure. I was pretty pessimistic myself. I kind of prided myself on it, actually. But I'd never met someone that burst with optimism like her.

I met her a few months before I moved in with my mother. I was still living with my previous girlfriend during our introduction, but that relationship was falling apart. Melodie was dating some chump in Idaho, but they weren't talking much. Is it bad to call the guy a chump? I mean, I never met him, but I didn't like him because whenever she talked about the dude, she wasn't so happy anymore, and that really said a lot about who he was. If someone is happy nonstop, and you have the power to make that person not so happy, well, I think that makes you a chump.

I stand by my assessment here.

We both worked at the hardware store. She was the gardening specialist and I was the assistant gardening manager, a title that at first sounded pretty grand, but I soon realized it only gave me the ability to tell people to do things, and when they said no, I had to go to the *real* department manager and complain. Then the department manager had to get involved and say, "Y'all need to listen to Clint" in this very maternal tone that seemed to say, "I'm disappointed in you." This happened a lot, actually, and it kind of reminded me of being an older brother who has to get his parents on the phone whenever he is left in charge because his siblings refuse to put on their pajamas.

Long story short, I wasn't exactly a great manager or a real source of authority.

I don't know if I ever have been, but that's a different story.

What I did have, however, was a fancy red vest, and that . . . Well, it made me feel something close to pride but not exactly prideful. It was an emotion pretty similar to how I'm sure the members of Jethro Tull felt after winning a Grammy over Metallica only for everyone to complain about it for 30 years.

On Mel's first day at the hardware store, I welcomed her and I introduced myself—and naturally, I made sure to include my title.

"I'm Clint, the, ahem, assistant manager. It's nice to meet you."

She shook my hand and said, "I'm Melodie

Venema."

I asked her to say her last name again. She repeated it slowly like she was used to the question, "VE-ne-MA."

I tried to say it again but didn't quite get it right, and so she stopped me and said, "It's like a combination of *venom* and *enema*."

"Whoa," I said. "That sounds dangerous."

And I kid you not, she winked in affirmation.

Then she said, "You can just call me Mel."

We started hanging out pretty regularly at work after that, and I don't know if it was because of the *venom* or the *enema*, but I couldn't help but find her interesting. Even when I was anxious, her presence just made me feel calmer. Her laugh was half nerdy, half adorable, and she often caught herself in the middle of a good chuckle and put her hand over her mouth and then went up on her toes in an attempt to stop herself. She was also incredibly smart, particularly when it came to plants.

She was a total plant nerd, something I'd never experienced and had no idea could be attractive. And I know—love at first sight, well, I don't know if that's a real thing. But when I was near Mel, I didn't think so much about the death of my father, which was still pretty fresh. I didn't think about the anxiety in my stomach or the fear that my OCD would come back. I didn't feel like I was failing at life, which was common for me at the time.

She was this intelligent, soft-spoken, always smiling, always funny, always charming, light.

I went out of my way to work with her. To talk to her. To engage with her. And as odd as this sounds, our first conversations weren't about work, or movies, or family, or any of that normal stuff people might talk about.

We mostly complained about who we were dating.

And I don't know if that's a good way to start a relationship. I don't know if that is recommended by dating experts. I'm not even sure if those people exist. Maybe they do online. I'll Google it later. But what I want to get at here is that as she described this dude who wasn't returning her calls, and was kind of avoiding her, and was not all that interesting, and was really into guns and camo and fast food, and who probably had a lot of body hair and smelled like sweat and farts and black powder, I couldn't help but put together a picture of who she was really looking for. And I felt like maybe, just maybe, I could be that person.

She wanted someone who made her laugh, and I had that down. I had her laughing *all* the time. She wanted someone who listened, and I thought what she had to say was very interesting. And I assumed she wanted someone who didn't smell like farts and gunpowder. I suppose it can be hard to assess that sort of thing, because smelling yourself can be a challenge, but as far as I could tell I smelled like Speed Stick—and sometimes Pop-Tarts in the morning—which felt like a step up in comparison to farts.

We started our relationship as coworkers, sure.

But then we became friends, and naturally, there was a part of me that wanted it to be more.

But I had these deep feelings of insecurity. I felt like this wonderfully happy, smiling-all-the-time, intelligent, thoughtful, beautiful-inside-and-out woman would never in a million years be interested in some anxious dude who was going nowhere, working at the hardware store in his early twenties and living with his mother.

I was a broken man, raised in a broken family, with a dead, drug-addicted dad. I mean, honestly, put all of that on a dating profile. I was the poster child for a "wounded dove." And sure, some women might be interested in men like that, but I didn't get that vibe from Mel. She came from a very wholesome Mormon working-class family, with parents who had been married for decades. To me, from her family to her disposition, she was the whole package, and I was a little nervous to enter a relationship with someone who was the whole package. Most of the girls I'd dated before had a few issues, same as I did. They had some emotional baggage, maybe some family trauma, and while that might not have helped the overall relationship, it did make me feel a little more comfortable being with them because it felt like we made sense.

We were both broken, and there is a lot of comfort in that.

But with Mel, I wondered if I'd just be the brick dragging her down.

And no one wants to be the brick.

So as much as I was interested in her, as much as I couldn't stop thinking about her, I kept it friendly.

But a couple of months after I moved in with my mother, as I was doing all this wavering and deep thinking and soul searching about Mel, trying to decide if I should ask her out, Mel asked if I'd found the note she left in my work vest several weeks earlier.

"What?" I asked.

Mel smiled, but at the same time she slightly shook her head like I was absolutely clueless and said, "I put a note in your vest a couple weeks ago. Just curious if you found it."

I immediately dug into my very classy assistant manager work vest like some oblivious idiot and sorted through all the receipts and random scraps of paper to find this note:

LET ME KNOW IF YOU WANT TO
GO OUT SOMETIME.

MEL

At the bottom of the note was her phone number.

I must have read that sucker a dozen times, and I couldn't help but pump my fist and cry to the heavens, "She likes me!" Which, I admit, was pretty juvenile. I felt the tingle of new romance from my fingers to my toes, but naturally I restrained myself because I was in a hardware store, and I was an assistant department manager, and I was pretty sure most of my coworkers thought I was crazy, and, well, they didn't need gas on that fire.

On our first date—if you could call it that—I helped Mel move a bike and a few boxes across town to her new apartment. It was nearly Thanksgiving, so after the move, we went out for pumpkin pie and hot chocolate at Village Inn, a coffee and pancake house. The place was kind of like a Denny's, if Denny's had a little brother that somehow smoked more cigarettes and drank more coffee than Denny's. We talked about her family and mine. Then we talked about her boyfriend in Idaho again.

"I started talking about marriage and he stopped returning my calls. I don't think we're dating anymore," she said.

Throughout most of our time together that night, Mel was always smiling. But at the mention of her boyfriend not calling her, she looked at the table, her lips twisted to the side.

She asked if I was afraid of marriage, which I will admit felt like a pretty progressive, foot-on-the-gas sort of question for a first date. I didn't know how to answer it. I didn't want to tell her that I was terrified of it. Mostly because mentally, I didn't know if I was well. Sure, I was functioning quite a bit better now. My OCD had downgraded to little more than occasional anxiety and self-loathing, but

I was terrified it would come back.

That's the odd thing about anxiety. There are these moments when it will downgrade, almost like a stalking ex who has stopped sending you threatening letters written in human blood for a month or two, and you think to yourself, *Good thing that's over.* And sure, that's comforting. I mean, who wants a threatening letter written in human blood? No one.

What I'm getting at is that once the anxiety and depression took a step back, I was relieved—but then I'd sit and wait, fearful that they were going to come back, which ultimately became another source of anxiety.

And when I thought about my anxiety coming back as full OCD, I wondered what would that do to a marriage. What would it do to my children? I was aware enough to know that I didn't want to bring more people into my mental baggage. But I also knew that there was something special about this person sitting across from me at that lowbrow pancake and coffee place, and I didn't want to ruin it.

So I told her something bland. Something that more or less diverted the question.

"I don't know," I said. "I try not to think about it."

It wasn't exactly a lie, I suppose, because I had thought about it. Quite a bit, and all of it terrified me. The honesty was in the "I try not to think about it." That was very true. I just wasn't all that good at not thinking about it.

She smiled, and later that night I asked if I

could kiss her.

She nodded, and we made out in my pickup for a while.

Which was awesome.

We started dating after that, and it wasn't long before Mel talked about us getting married. And wow, was I conflicted. It's so hard to describe the light that she brought into my life. With my anxiety and my occasional depression, life seemed so dark. I didn't think much about the future, I just thought about getting through the day without a panic attack. But with Mel, the lights came on. The sunlight broke through the trees. There was a glow to her that gave me feelings of hope and peace that I'd only felt from one other person.

My grandmother.

And maybe that's weird to compare a woman you are in love with to your grandmother. I mean, they didn't look all that much alike. It was more their presence. The same way that my grandmother made me feel safe Mel made me feel hopeful. She made me feel like there was potential for a better life ahead, which at this time was like some magical fairy dust sprinkled from a real-life unicorn who just spent the day sliding down a rainbow.

I know this all sounds very flowery, and a little mythical, but it's the reality of how I felt. I'll just say it: I wanted to be a better person with Mel in my life. I wanted to work harder. I wanted to find a path in life and be something more than I was. Sure, I'd thought about marriage before meeting her, but with Mel it was different. It was always with this pinch of terror, and it wasn't how my friends felt terror when thinking about marriage. It wasn't the responsibility that scared me. It was myself that I was afraid of.

I thought about my parents' nasty divorce and realized I didn't want to experience anything like that again, regardless of which side of the equation I was on. I wondered if I was capable of being in a healthy relationship because of my mental illness. Part of me wondered if my DNA was bad, while another part wondered if it would be best to just get sterilized now and not bring more mental illness into the world.

I wanted to be with Mel, but saying "I do" felt a lot like listing "Can speak Spanish" on a job application when I really couldn't.

I'd get the job, and then stand there like an idiot, everyone speaking perfectly good Spanish while I just nodded along, faking it until someone pointed at me and screamed, "He can't speak Spanish!" And I'd just smile and nod because they said it in Spanish. Only it wouldn't be a job, it would be a marriage. Losing a job for lying on the application would really affect only me. Well, and the employer. But I stand by my simile.

Anyway, getting married when I wasn't mentally able to function as a loving husband would affect Mel, and that seemed irresponsible, because the fact was I'd fallen head over heels in love with her. I couldn't find the willpower to break up with her, but I also couldn't seem to find the words to fully tell her about my anxiety because I thought it might scare her away.

Not telling Mel about my anxiety was complex, particularly when I consider that I didn't fully understand it myself. I wasn't sure if it was gone, or still in me. I was living a more stable life now. So I told her only what I had to. Which was exactly what I told everyone else: "I sometimes get anxious at night." And when I think back on that statement, I feel like I was following my mother's example of never saying too much about your mental illness. I had fallen into my mother's code of silence in this new relationship. When I think about that, I realize how much her example impacted my actions, but it also makes me realize why she made the decision to keep things quiet.

Like me, Mom didn't want to scare people away, and she didn't want to be judged.

One thing was for sure: Just thinking about all of this caused me a lot of anxiety, because anxiety is a horrible loop that feeds on itself until you have to pull the car over while on a date and throw up in a Burger King bathroom and then tell some crazy story about a kid throwing up on you in the restroom as you try to explain the puke on your jeans (true story).

Around this time, I was trying to get out of the hardware store, and a friend of mine recently got a job as a prison guard. The money was good, along with the benefits. He said it was mostly sitting around. Well, outside of the times when you fear for your life because, you know, you're working at a prison. I did all the testing. I somehow passed the psychological evaluation, which seems crazy to me considering I basically lied the whole time. But I knew all the deception was going to come to a head soon, because my last step in the interview process included a polygraph test—they were going to ask me the same questions they'd asked me in the psychological test to see if I was lying.

The morning of the polygraph test, I stopped at a light as I was about to get on the freeway, and I asked myself if I really wanted to work in a prison. I also had a pretty strong feeling that there was no way I'd pass the polygraph test. And then I thought about Mel. In the time it took for the light to change, I switched my blinker, turned south instead of north, and drove to that same open-enrollment college I tried to attend almost three years earlier. I parked in front of the school, walked to the welcome desk, and said, "I'd like to be a student here again. How do I do that?"

The people at the welcome desk sent me to an advising office, and I asked those people the same question. I asked that question to what felt like a dozen people that day, and by that evening, I was a college student again. I went straight to Mel's apartment and told her what I'd done—and how I was absolutely terrified.

I gave her my reasons.

First, I didn't know how to type. Or at least not very well. I mean, I had my two index fingers down, but the other eight fingers really weren't all that involved or interested in typing. I'd never finished reading a novel. I'd barely graduated high school. I'd already dropped out of college once, and in the words of my grandmother, I wasn't exactly "a go-getter." I was more of a "Let's go get a pizza and *not* talk about how I have no plans for the future" kinda guy.

But there was something about Mel that made me want to be so much more, and I thought of her as I walked into that college and walked out a student. She was my strength. At that moment, she was my motivation.

I went on ranting to Mel about this list of reasons why I wasn't sure how I was going to ever graduate from college, and ended it with, "I can't even speak casually without using a swear or making fart jokes. This was so stupid."

I expected her to call me a chump, or a scrub, or a pathetic man-child.

But she didn't laugh at me. What she did say, in this simple, reassuring way was, "I'll help you."

My first semester, I handwrote all my papers on a notepad. Then I sat next to Mel in her one-bedroom apartment with its broken furnace and read as she typed, because my handwriting and spelling were so bad she couldn't read what I'd written.

Naturally, this lasted only one semester until Mel got sick of typing all my papers and flatly said, "You're going to need to figure this out." But that offer to help me, well, it never stopped. Mel had recently finished an associate's degree in Idaho, so she became my guide to college, and I simply marveled at her clear and thoughtful answers and her total willingness to help me do something I didn't think I could ever do on my own. And her help, her simple investment in me as I tried to better myself, was easily the best gift I'd ever received. I kinda gushed over how amazing she was, and thoughtful, and smart . . .

As she helped me understand college, I fell deeper in love with her.

But the real kicker was when I introduced Mel to Grandma. She lived at a nursing home in east Provo. She struggled with dementia. Sometimes she would be coherent and understanding, the same Grandma who told me to cut my hair (and yes, by this time I had cut my hair) and comforted me about my poop-haps and said things like, "How was work, sweetie?" or, "Oh, I am so happy to see you."

Other times she called out for an old cousin that I'd never met, her face a twisted mixture of terror and confusion. "Madge, Madge, what are we going to do? What are we going to do, Madge?"

I hated seeing her in that place, and I hated seeing her struggling with her own madness, but what I hated the most was thinking of her in there alone, so I visited her every day, never knowing what to expect but always crossing my fingers that she would greet me with that same old smile and spark of recognition.

Grandma was not her usual self the day she met Mel, but she wasn't lost in her own mind either. It was evening. She was in bed, lying on her side, facing the door. The room was dark but for a brass desk lamp that sat on a wooden side table. The room was small, just large enough for the bed, the table, and a pink rocker. She wasn't wearing her teeth, and her curly hair, usually dyed brown, was matted on all sides, the roots gray. I asked how her day had gone and asked if she had a good dinner. I told her that I loved her and then I introduced Mel. Grandma said little outside of yes and no. She nodded a couple of times, but mostly she closed her eyes and listened.

After a moment of silence, Grandma reached out and gripped my hand. Then, with great struggle, she reached out and gripped Mel's. She put our hands together, gave us this gap-toothed smile, and said, "She's a good one. Thank you for bringing a good one home to your grandmother."

Then she rolled over and went to sleep.

Years earlier, when I was sixteen, I introduced her to a girl, and Grandma took me into another room and whispered, "She's trash. Why would you bring this trash home to meet your grandmother?" Two months later, as I was working at Pizza Hut, that same girl got into an argument with one of my coworkers and threw a chair from the lobby at her head.

So yeah, Grandma was sorta right. And in the case of Mel, she was also right. She was "a good one," and although I was terrified that I couldn't be the husband I wanted to be, and I was weighted with the shadow of my parents' messy divorce, Grandma's endorsement helped me make the decision.

I would ask Mel to marry me.

A few months before I proposed, Grandma died in that same care center. Aunts, cousins, the whole family surrounded her in this cramped room as she struggled to take her final breaths. My aunt pulled me to the front of the group, looked me in the eyes, and said, "Tell her it's okay to go. Tell her you will be okay." I stood over Grandma, realizing that this moment, her passing, was one of my greatest fears.

For so long, she was all I had.

But I didn't feel as scared as I always assumed I would, and I think it's because I had Mel in the waiting room. I had someone in my life, and this isn't to say that I didn't need my grandmother anymore. I think I will always need her. Right now, as I write this sentence years later, I can't think of a day that I haven't thought about Grandma. But I knew that, with Mel and the changes I'd made and the path I was on, I could make it in this life without her. And as I looked at Grandma clinging to life in that hospital bed and listened to her short, shallow breaths and the beeps of the monitors that were steadily slowing, I knew clearly that her time with me was at an end.

But I knew that I'd never have made it here, to this point of independence, if she hadn't been there for me when I needed someone most.

I leaned over Grandma, her breaths choppy and inconsistent, her face pale, and I whispered, "It's okay, Grandma. You can go. I'm going to be okay."

She stopped breathing moments later.

I left the room, almost dizzy. I sat next to Mel

in the waiting room, and I cried as Mel held me.

Four months after that moment, I asked Mel to marry me.

With a glowing, radiant smile, she agreed.

A FEELING
I HADN'T EXPECTED

Two years into our marriage, and Mel and I were living in Provo, less than a mile from my grandmother's old home, renting a small two-bedroom farmhouse owned by a family friend. What we discussed more than any other topic, at least twice a day, was having a baby.

I suppose we'd talked about having a child while dating, but it was mostly playful. We talked about what the child would look like: Would he be short and stocky like me, or short and slender like Mel. We talked about our child's personality: Would she be funny and jittery like me, or reserved and thoughtful like Mel?

We picked out names.

But it didn't seem all that real until Mel said, "I think we should start trying."

It was early evening, and Mel and I were making dinner in our impossibly small kitchen, me working in front of the dishwasher, Mel crammed next to the stove, both of us throwing elbows for counter space.

"Trying what?" I asked.

"Having a baby."

"Whoa, my friend. Slow down," I said. "I think we need to wait."

Mel went on, coming at the conversation head-on, taking no prisoners, asking me why we needed to wait, why we needed to slow down.

"We love each other, right? We are married. There's no reason to wait," she said.

I agreed with her on the fact that we were married and in love. I was very much in love with her. But I told her that we needed to become a little more accustomed to being a married couple. We needed to save money. We needed to be securer. We needed to be older, and wiser, and more established. I was still in college, probably two years away from graduating.

And we were, in fact, very young. We were both 23, and while at the time I felt very old and mature and knowledgeable about the world, while I held a pretty clear understanding of what was important in life, the reality was that I was an immature man-child. I'd never voted in an election because I just didn't "have time for politics," which basically meant I didn't watch the news or read the paper, but I could go on for days with my suspicions about who was actually behind the Dharma Initiative on the show *Lost*. To my credit, however, I had recently signed a petition for a movement I was very passionate about: bringing back the animated show *Futurama*. I suppose what I'm trying to get at here is that I was old enough to get married, to love my spouse, to pay my bills, and to pass my classes.

But I had no real understanding of the world and my priorities were a little out of line, and if I were to take everything I knew about the world and life and put it in a bucket, it would maybe be half full. *Maybe.* But I'm a pessimist, so I suppose it would be half empty, and going into parenthood with a half-empty bucket didn't feel right.

"Can't we wait until I'm done with school?" I asked.

I brought up a bunch of cliché arguments as to why I didn't want to have a baby yet, and Mel had an answer for all of them. Every single one, because she'd obviously prepared for this moment. She'd done her homework, bringing up that we had family close, so they could help with the baby while I finished school. She went on about how we were nearly two years into marriage, and we had a good relationship, and we had insurance through my university.

Every single argument I presented she had an answer for, but my whole argument—all of it—was a smoke show.

Yeah, those other arguments about waiting until we were more established were real. I mean, I thought about them. But they were secondary on my overall list of reasons I felt I should never in a million years have a child.

First and foremost, I was afraid I'd pass on my mental illness. I thought about that a lot, actually. I didn't really understand how genetics worked. I didn't know if having mental illness was nature or nurture, but I couldn't help wondering if maybe along with my brown hair, blue eyes, and stocky frame, I'd also pass down the real whopper: my anxiety disorder. And that thought made me want to just get sterilized, to take myself out of the possible gene pool, because I couldn't think of anything worse to give my child.

I was also afraid I wouldn't know how to be a good father because I never had an active father. I was still worried that I'd end up pulling some of the same moves my dad pulled, and I think a lot of that has to do with the fact that I didn't really understand why he acted the way he did. I mean, I knew him. But I didn't know him well enough to be able to look at his life and say, "There it is. That was the turning point. That was the huge mistake he made, and that's what I need to avoid." I feared that I would somehow absentmindedly walk right into the same trap he did, almost like my genetics were a compass forced to point down the same path, that it was just a matter of time before they fully kicked in, and suddenly I'd find myself toothless and dead in a small apartment, my own child trying to make sense of the loss.

But sadly, the biggest fear I had, the one that trumped them all, was that if we had a child, I would be forced to get up at night, which would break my bedtime routine and cause me to have panic attacks. I'd gotten pretty good at molding my anxiety around my life, getting up around the same time, going to classes around the same time, going to work around the same time, and hitting the gym somewhere in the middle. Any disruption to my sleep or my schedule sent me into a rambling anxious fit.

Sure, I was living a much more normal life than a few years ago. And from a bird's-eye view, I looked pretty normal. I was managing my obligations, and doing well in school, and trying to be a good husband. But that anxiety . . . It was still there, in the corner of my existence, like a snoozing monster that could, at any moment, stir—and each time it did, I was so afraid that I might not get it back to sleep again.

I thought about Mel going into labor in the middle of the night and how it might bring on a panic attack, and I wondered if my anxiety would prevent me from being there for her during a moment when I absolutely needed to be there for her.

I thought about how I'd more or less quit medications outside of one or two that I took occasionally, once a month or less when I absolutely needed it. Other than that, I avoided any medications like they were a dirty, nasty sin. I wondered if having a child might force me to go back, guns blazing, to handfuls of pills each day, and that thought, when I remembered my father's addiction, felt like a slippery slope.

I suppose the real question that I couldn't shake was: Would having a child undo all that I'd done to get my OCD under control? I was terrified of having a setback, and when I think about that, I realize that I was once again allowing my anxiety to make decisions for me. It felt like I was trying not to have a child because doing so might bring back my anxiety, and that anxiety might prevent me from being the father I wanted and needed to be, and the thought of doing that to my child felt like I was becoming my father. And all of that potential conflict between my anxiety and my desire to be a better father than the one I had was a road I didn't know if I was strong enough to go down.

And so, like I often did at this time, I sat by myself, trying to understand these feelings, allowing them to turn and bubble in my head until I felt sick to my stomach but never knowing how to explain them to Mel.

We went back and forth on the subject of having a baby for months. And at first, it was playful, but it was also clear that she wanted a baby more than anything in the world.

We'd be going out on a date, and I'd say, "What do you want to do tonight?"

And she'd say, "Have a baby."

That was her canned response to a lot of my questions, actually.

"Where do you want to go after work?"

"I want to have a baby."

"What should we make for dinner?"

"How about we skip dinner and make a baby?"

I kept to my pitch. I kept to my reasoning that we needed to understand each other better and become more established and blah, blah, blah, and Mel wasn't buying it. She knew me well enough to know that I wasn't being 100 percent truthful with her. She could see it in my eyes, my hesitation, my stutter. And yet when she'd say, "What's the real reason?" I always stuck to my story.

And part of the real struggle was this: I didn't know how to tell her in a way that would sound rational or logical or even close to sane. I knew all of this was in my head. But that didn't make it any less real.

I couldn't help but think back to when my OCD was at its worst. There were a couple of times when close friends asked what was going on with me. They asked why I never hung out anymore and why I was so motivated to exercise. I tried to be open about my fear of sleep and anxiety, and tried to put it into sentences, but the moment my explanation touched the air, it turned sour. It all sounded so irrational, even to me, and yet it was very real and painful inside my body. I often wondered if there was some disconnect between fear and logic inside my mind, and I still felt self-conscious when discussing my anxiety with anyone, even Mel.

I think I had fears that made sense only to me, and trying to explain them to Mel, this woman I loved so deeply, made me worry that she'd finally realize that I was flat-out crazy. Mel was so level, so balanced. She was charming, and normal, while I felt odd and scared and confused and depressed. One of the things I loved the most about her was how calm and logical she was. These were traits I didn't feel I had in myself, and I was afraid that if I showed her the full weight of my mental illness, she'd realize that this relationship really wasn't right for her.

I couldn't think of a thicker, heavier, frothier failure to swallow than to scare her with my anxiety and cause her to leave.

It wasn't until things got heated and the playful banter became arguments that I finally brought up my real reasoning.

Mel knew about my anxiety, but she'd never seen the brunt of it. I'd had a few attacks while with her, but often my anxiety flared while she was asleep, so I was able to keep it to myself. I'd never had a full-blown, weeks-long anxiety spell since we'd been married, and I was grateful.

I explained my fears as best I could, and Mel didn't call me crazy. She didn't look at me like she'd made a bad decision in getting married. All she said was, "I will get up at night with the baby. I will take care of that. Don't worry about it." She said it with absolute sincerity and conviction.

She was 100 percent serious.

When Mel told me this, I felt a little better. But I knew the truth. I knew that if we had a child, I needed to help at night. I couldn't avoid it, nor did I think it was right for me to avoid it. I thought a lot about my father and how he wasn't around, and I felt a strong sense of duty. If we had a child, I needed to be there. Every hour of every day. I needed to be fully committed. I refused to be in and out of my child's life, like my father had been in and out of mine. But the thought of that duty felt like I was at war with my anxiety, and I feared that I didn't have it in me. I feared that somehow my anxiety would get in the way, make me incapable of being the kind of father I wanted to be, and that was easily one of the worst fears of my life.

But there was the other fear.

What if I passed on my anxiety?

Finally I said, "No. I can't do that. I have to be there for you, for us. I'm just . . . What if our child . . ." I struggled to say it, but finally it came out. "What if our child is like me?"

I looked at Mel with absolute dread. What if, somehow, I'd make someone like me, and that someone would have my same anxiety, my same pain inside. I didn't want that. I wanted that pain to end with me. But before I had a chance to explain further, Mel said, "I'm hoping for it."

She said it with a full smile, like she'd thought about this before. She'd thought about it a lot, actually. I could see that in her eyes. She said it like I had something great to offer. Like a child like me was something she actually desired. I didn't know if it was my personality, or my drive, or my charm . . . I didn't know the specific attributes that she was hoping I'd pass on, but it definitely wasn't my anxiety. She didn't seem worried about that at all. It was a view of myself I'd never seen before in another person. It was pure, absolute love and admiration for what I had to offer. My anxiety wasn't even a consideration. Through her eyes I saw something in myself that was worth giving to my children, and although I couldn't see it in myself, it was right there, in the eyes of my wife.

And suddenly I didn't feel so afraid anymore, almost like that confidence she had in my ability to be a father was bleeding into me, and it was the best gift anyone had ever given me.

The moment Mel said, "I'm hoping for it" was the turning point. It was the moment that made me feel like maybe I could be a father.

It was seeing myself through her eyes that did it.

The day Mel showed me the positive pregnancy test, I felt like the biggest test of my life was only a few months away. Mel was jumping for joy, smiling, hugging me. Kissing me. Her brown hair bouncing as she leapt, her fists clenched, her whole body showing nothing but complete excitement. Then, as she called her sister and her mother to tell them the good news, I quietly went into the bathroom, locked the door, and cried.

And then I prayed.

I asked God to please help me find the strength to be something more than my father. Then I prayed that He could make me something more than myself. I prayed every night afterward for the Lord to make me strong enough. That He take away my anxiety so that I could be there for my child. I don't know if I'd ever prayed so hard in my life.

The day finally came two weeks earlier than expected. Mel came down with preeclampsia, which made her ankles, feet, and face swell. She went to visit with her doctor one morning, only to be taken straight to the delivery room for an emergency cesarean. I was scared for Mel and the baby, but the doctor assured us that everything was going to be fine.

And once everything was said and done, I was excited to hold my son, but more than anything, I was relieved that it didn't happen in the night. And when I think about all the joy of having a baby, and how much I love and value my son, I feel selfish for being more relieved by the time of day that he was born than excited by the miracle of birth.

That first night was a long one. We were in a small hospital room, Mel in a white hospital bed, half propped up, while I was given a turquoise, slippery plastic chair that folded out into a single bed. It was the most restless night I'd had in years, and I admit that I took a Xanax for the first time in a very long time. I felt terrible about it, and I wondered if this was the beginning of my downfall.

The nurse left Tristan in Mel's room, because after trying for most of the night, she couldn't get him to sleep. He refused to sleep, and it felt like my fear of his not sleeping and keeping me awake was coming true. I waited for the inevitable pit in my gut, and cold sweats, and nausea. And there was part of me, the fearful, anxiety-fueled part, that wanted to run out of the hospital room. I wanted to just get in my truck and drive home. Another part of me wanted to hit the pills, take them all, until I got so numb I couldn't feel anything anymore—not the anxiety, not even the joy of this life-changing moment.

But then I looked at Mel, in the hospital bed, her brown hair pulled back, with several loose strands falling into her face, sleeping soundly for the first time since giving birth. I loved her. I knew I did. From my hair to my toes. And to be real, her cesarean was the scariest thing I'd ever witnessed. They literally cut her open and took out a screaming, bloody human.

People always described childbirth to me in these grand, wonderful statements. They told me it was magical, and it changes a person's life. And all of that is true. But no one told me the actual act of giving birth would look like I was on the set of John Carpenter's *The Thing*. It was not magical or wonderful, but terrifying and sticky, with lots of vacuums sucking out body fluid. I got weak at the knees just looking at the business end and had to sit down to keep from throwing up. Mel was all sorts of badass for going through it, and by the end, I knew without a shadow of a doubt that she was the toughest person I'd ever met.

And yet there I was, wanting to run away from the whole thing because of my anxiety.

There was a part of me—the logical part—that knew if Mel was strong enough to go through childbirth, I could make it through the first night with our new son.

And the more I thought about running, the more it felt like something my father would do. So I stopped, and breathed, and I held my son as he cried and Mel slept. And somehow, this sense of duty, these feelings of knowing that I had to be there for my wife, my son, my new family of three, overshadowed my nighttime anxiety.

I was flooded with a sense of duty. It didn't make the anxiety go away. Not completely. But it gave me enough strength to tamp it down so that I could be there for my family.

About 5:00 a.m., I was holding Tristan while Mel slept. He was awake, swaddled in a blanket. For nearly thirty minutes he'd been quiet. This was a record for his first night. The sun was coming up, and I'd done little more than doze here and there between his cries.

It was just light enough in the room for me to see Tristan's smooth face and dark eyes. During all his struggling and crying, Tristan had managed to work his right arm loose from the tightly wrapped blanket. He reached up and gripped my right index finger with a wrinkled pink hand. His whole hand wasn't much bigger than the tip of my finger.

We looked at each other for a while. His pupils were dark, soft face curious.

It was so late.

It was so early.

It was quiet.

Somehow I knew that we were in this together. I knew that he needed me, but I also needed him.

I don't remember falling asleep, but I remember sleeping deeply.

When I awoke, the sun was up, a nurse was in the room, Mel was still asleep, and Tristan was peacefully sleeping in the crook of my arm, his hand still gripping my finger, never letting go. I remember feeling like I'd accomplished some great feat by getting Tristan to fall asleep for a few hours, and all it had taken was my index finger. Somehow, with the simple grip of my son's small hand, I knew that everything was going to be okay as long as I held him, cared for him, and loved him.

During the excitement of having a baby, I hadn't taken the time to realize that I was now a father. One of my biggest fears was taking place and I was still alive. And Tristan was still alive. And Mel was still alive. I was still scared of making the same mistakes my father had made, and I was still nervous about how the demands of raising a baby might impact my anxiety.

But there was a new feeling that I hadn't expected: hope.

WHEN FEELINGS OF FAILURE ARE IN VOGUE

I was always searching out praise, and it drove my professors nuts. I was a very needy English major. I was that student who hung out after class to chat, fishing for compliments, to the point that professors avoided me on sight, darting out of the classroom before I had a chance to approach them. I remember one poetry professor, a balding and slightly pudgy chain-smoker with a PhD who was somehow still kind of suave, with his argyle sweaters and thick-framed glasses, putting his hand up as I approached after class and saying, "I'd love to get home at a decent hour today, so why don't you go fish for compliments from one of my colleagues?"

I stood there and laughed a little, hopeful that he was joking. Surely he was kidding, right? I wasn't irritating enough for him to shoo me off so flatly. He was just pulling my leg. Any moment he'd laugh, and then we'd chat about how awesome my analysis of "Kubla Khan" was. But he didn't say another word. He just stood there and stared at me, not speaking until I put my head down and walked away.

But I didn't go home.

Instead, I took his advice and went into the faculty hallway to chat with another professor, fishing for more praise. And as I did, it seemed like the others could sense I was coming, because as I walked down the hall, office doors began to shut. So I went to the campus gym and lifted weights, the whole time feeling like I was failing at life, and school, and marriage, and everything I touched.

But if I stood back and thought about how I made the dean's list each and every semester, there really wasn't much room to say I was failing. As far as I could tell, Mel and I were happy in our marriage. We were three years in, with a son. We still laughed a lot. We were making ends meet. Sure, it was stressful having a child while finishing school. And yeah, we argued from time to time, as all new couples do, but it wasn't a common occurrence. I don't think there was a day that went by when we didn't say we loved each other. We were even one of those couples that, after a fight, would still go to bed together and then grudgingly say, "I love you" through tense lips before turning our backs to each other. I was working as a server at a chain restaurant, and Mel was working at a different big-box hardware store than the one where we met. We were figuring each other out as a couple and as parents.

And you know what, we weren't doing half bad.

Yet feelings of failure were my default, and I couldn't seem to shake them, so to take my mind off my own inadequacies, I lifted weights endlessly, falling back into my old habit of overexercising.

They say anxiety, mental illness, and depression change with age. I was in my mid-twenties, and suddenly I felt like I was failing, despite all the evidence to the contrary.

This was my new anxiety.

It was the new pit in my stomach.

It was the reason I couldn't sleep at night. (Well, outside of having a child.)

Failure greeted me in the morning, and failure tucked me into bed at night.

And when I look back at this time, I can see that much of this was impostor syndrome. I didn't feel like I belonged in college. My parents didn't go to college nor did my grandparents. I was the definition of a first-generation student. When I told my mother I was going back to school, she laughed and said "You've never been very good at that. Why don't you just try to get a good job with the city?" I came from a long line of farmers, trade workers, and municipal employees, so the thought of going to college, even an open-enrollment state college, made my family look at me like I was out of my mind. My older brother earned a college degree, and he was seen as an oddball. But he studied computer something or other, which somehow made his time in school a more worthwhile pursuit.

I was wasting time and money studying English. I might as well have been getting a degree in underwater basket weaving, a made-up degree that my stepfather, mother, non-college-degree-seeking friends—the whole wad—used as a comparison, each one of them acting like they were so original, laughing to themselves about how funny they were with their made-up useless degree name, when in fact they were nothing more than a huge cliché. But regardless of their lack of originality, I felt like an outcast around family and friends because I was in college, something they didn't understand. And at school, I felt like I didn't belong because of the family I came from.

I kept waiting to be pulled out of class by some group of administrators in suits, all of them with a Big Brother vibe, perhaps along with a campus officer, one of those dudes that zipped along the campus hallways on a Segway, trying to look like he held some authority—but he was on a Segway, so any authority he held was void. He'd say, "I'm sorry, son. We made a mistake. You don't belong here." They'd put me in handcuffs, and take me away, and everyone from the students to the instructors would sigh in unanimous relief, one or two would clap, and everyone would think to themselves, *Yes! Finally, someone took action. Someone finally noticed that Clint did not belong here.*

And I knew that would never happen, but it felt like it *should* happen, so I was always seeking out confirmation that I belonged. Good grades, comprehension, more classes, more concept mastery, none of it filled the void I felt inside that seemed to say, "Get out of here, you fraud." I felt like I was just some outsider looking in, and it all translated into my feeling like a failure despite my successes in the classroom.

I have a feeling that if I were meeting with a therapist at this time, they would have told me all of it was my inner child looking for external praise or confirmation that I was doing well because I didn't get a lot of that from my parents. I'm sure little Clint was in there, pulling at my subconscious like it was a jump rope, screaming, "Tell me I belong! Help me feel like I have value!" But I didn't understand that sort of thing yet, because the thought of meeting with a therapist—or any doctor—freaked me out. After my dad died, I decided that doctors, therapists, the whole medical establishment was to be used as little as possible. I mean, sure I went to a doctor if I had strep throat or something, but meeting regularly with any doctor or therapist felt like a step back to becoming my dad, a step back to abusing doctors and abusing medications. So I was determined to not seek help for my mental illness.

Rather, I just sat in the classroom, an anxious mess, looking like a totally normal college student on the outside but feeling like a fraud on the inside and trying desperately to hide those feelings. I was a Hot Pocket that was cooked to perfection on the outside—all crispy, flaky goodness—but I was still frozen in the middle. And you know what? No one likes their Hot Pockets like that.

I had similar feelings in my marriage. I felt like I didn't know what I was doing or how to be a good husband, so I tried as hard as I could, but I was also waiting for Mel to pull me into the kitchen and say, "I made a huge mistake." I pulled the same moves with her, seeking out confirmation that I belonged in this marriage, and all of this made me come across as very needy.

Poor Mel, bless her wonderful and thoughtful heart. I'd sit across from her and ask if I was a good husband. I asked if she still loved me. If she still found me charming and attractive and funny. And she'd say, "Yes. I think you are all of those things." And then I'd ask her again a week or two later, and she'd agree, only for me to not believe her. I don't want to say that I followed her around like a puppy, asking for snacks and belly rubs, but it was pretty clear that my confidence was lacking—and from everything I've read about what women find attractive, confidence is key, and I had little.

In my brain, I was somehow aware of this breakdown between my self-worth and actual fact, yet I couldn't seem to stop questioning my value and asking for reassurance, and that caused me to wonder if my fear of failure was going to ruin my marriage, which ultimately only exacerbated the fear, almost like a self-fulfilling prophecy.

Which is totally in the anxiety playbook.

Anxiety is such a feeding-on-itself little dick-head that develops its own tics, and then it uses those tics to make you more anxious, like some sort of perpetual anxiety motion machine that turns and bubbles in your gut until you end up eating a bacon and butter sandwich because it reminds you of your grandmother, and that's a source of comfort. But then your wife comes into the kitchen, the air heavy with bacon smoke, and she can't understand why on earth anyone would eat something like that, and you end up feeling like a failure again.

And I think the worst part of it was the ruminating thoughts. I'd sit up at 2:00 a.m. and think about mistakes, bad conversations, moments when I said something stupid or looked stupid. And I thought about how everyone, every single person I knew—from professors, to friends, to coworkers, to my own very wonderful wife—assumed I was an idiot, unqualified, a huge failure, and I didn't belong. I'd replay interactions in my head that were totally normal, completely forgettable to everyone else but me and kick myself over something I said or should have said, something I did or didn't do, until I couldn't sleep, and couldn't eat, and couldn't feel anything else but shame and failure, and every muscle in my body was tight and exhausted, and my gut was a ball of anxious butterflies trying to break out of my body.

During this time, I also turned to my faith. When Mel and I met, we were both pretty room temperature regarding Mormonism. But once we started talking seriously about marriage, we made a decision to become more active. We were married in a Mormon temple, which was kind of a big deal for us, and our families, and most of our other Mormon friends.

Each night I prayed to not feel like such a failure, and each morning, I woke up with the same old depressed feelings. I constantly asked God to reach into my head and twist a bolt or uncross a wire. I mean, come on. How hard would that be for God to do? Yeah, sure, he had big important things to do, but maybe on his lunch break, or just after breakfast but before he got on Facebook? Surely God could find the time to fix my mental illness. Right?

It's not like I was asking him to regrow a limb or anything. I wasn't asking him to give me a new eyeball or cure my leprosy. I just didn't want to feel like an anxious failure when I knew, logically, I wasn't.

But God never fixed it.

Or maybe I should say, he didn't answer my prayers. Although that sounds harsh. God had answered many of my prayers. Mel, for example, was incredible. She was as much of a light in my life as my grandmother once was. And our son, although exhausting, was an amazing blessing. I had overcome so much, and I honestly wonder if what I was most afraid of was going backward. Back to that old life I had as a child, when everything seemed so uncertain and I had no control over the difficult situations around me.

There was something about bad things happening when I was young that made me wait for the next bad thing to happen, even when good things were happening. Almost like I couldn't savor the successes because I knew, just around the corner, was the next letdown. I couldn't help but wonder if I was going to absentmindedly

ANXIOUSLY EVER AFTER

become the source of that next bad thing, and that
translated into my wondering if I was doing it all
wrong, if I was actually failing instead of moving
steadily away from the hardships of my childhood.

But I didn't really understand any of that well
enough to put into a paragraph, so I prayed for
help, and in a lot ways, it felt like what I was
really doing was trying to find control. I wanted
the assurance that bad things wouldn't happen,
which in life isn't something you can always have,
and the simple uncertainty of not knowing if I'd be
successful in marriage, or college, or parenthood—
or anything really—filled me with dread.

And when it got bad enough that suicidal
ideation was once again a daily occurrence, I
went to see my Mormon bishop for a blessing for
the sick.

So here's how all that works: Mormons believe in
a divine priesthood, and one of the fringe benefits
of the priesthood is blessing the sick and afflicted,
same as Christ did with lepers and the blind.

Last time I read the New Testament, though, I
didn't notice Christ taking a grown man, putting
his hands on him, and saying, "I cure you of your
irrational anxiety and fear of failure," after which
the man got up and walked around, feeling like a
million Roman coins.

And to be fair, this was probably 2006, and
mental illness, well, it still wasn't talked about all
that much, particularly within the Mormon church.
It was still seen as an all-in-your-head sort of thing,
not a real illness. It was just a get-over-it illness.

I suppose I even felt that way myself. I was still living a mostly drug-free life, without any therapy, and living that way made me feel like I had control over my anxiety. But looking back at how needy I was and how often I sought out praise and felt anxious about every stupid little mistake, from getting a bad quiz score to messing up an order at my restaurant job, kicking myself nonstop until I experienced those old nauseous feelings, it was clear that I didn't have any control over my emotions and really needed therapy. But I saw going back to therapy as a step back, and going back instead of forward was a huge source of anxiety.

So rather than confide in my wife or seek out medical help (because doctors still terrified me), I turned to faith because, you know, God is good, and he'd have my back, even if what I was dealing with didn't make any sense to anyone but me. And yeah, it felt pretty good talking to God about my problems. He's a good listener, for sure. But I wasn't getting better, so I decided maybe what I needed were the big guns.

I needed a Mormon blessing for the sick from my local bishop.

But that would mean confiding in someone about how I was feeling and what was going on in my head, which was scary in and of itself, particularly for anyone struggling with mental illness. Finally, when things became too much, I made an appointment to meet with the bishop after church.

He was a slender, almost ropy, balding man who wore big, square, 1990s-style glasses that darkened in the sunlight. He wore a white shirt and a brown suit with a braided leather and brass bull-shaped bolo tie, cowboy boots, and western-style pants. To be honest, he reminded me of an oil tycoon. You know, the kind of guy who might retire in Texas and drive a white convertible Cadillac with gold trim and some bullhorns mounted to the front.

Mormons don't have paid clergy, so he earned his living working with metal part-time and farming the rest of the time. With calloused hands and slightly bowed legs, he looked a lot like many men in that part of Utah. He was a root-tootin' dude in his early fifties, the same age my father would have been had he not died.

He smiled and asked what I needed help with.

And once I was there, across from him in his office, looking down the barrel of his bolo tie and tough-guy gaze, I struggled to speak. I had a strong feeling he wasn't going to take me seriously. His overall vibe was that he spent weekends wrapping bears in sleeper holds and then putting their unconscious bodies in charming poses for a memorable photo shoot.

I was going to chat with him about my anxiety problem?

My feelings of failure?

My crippling insecurities?

I knew it was a bad idea the moment I sat in his church office, but I was so miserable, and I needed help, and he was a man of God.

I began with a string of *umms*, but eventually it came out.

"I'm wondering if you could give me a blessing for the sick," I said.

"Okay," he said with this slight rural Utah twang. "What's troubling ya?"

"My anxiety," I said

Or at least that was the gist of it. I might have added some more descriptive verbs in there. Like "soul-crushing anxiety" or maybe "anxious feelings of failure that sometimes make me cry in the bathtub." You know, something to let him know the severity of the situation.

Then I closed my eyes because I was about to cry in front of this masculine character. I just wanted the Lord's help so badly.

He didn't console me or tell me he understood.

Instead, he snickered to himself. Then he buttoned it up and told me that being anxious doesn't mean you're sick. It means you need to toughen up. "You can't be going around telling people stuff like that," he said, "You do understand that, don't ya?"

Suddenly he gave me this long-winded lecture on masculinity, which to be honest, was not the reason I came in.

Not. At. All.

But I suppose I should have expected it. In his own way, he was trying to help. He knew I didn't have much of a father in my life, and I think he was trying to help me understand how to engage the world the way he did, with the toughness of a slice of well-aged beef jerky.

He said I really didn't need a blessing for the sick and suggested I drink more water and go camping. "Whenever I don't feel right," he said. "I just get out there, in the woods, and the fresh air soothes my soul." He looked out the window with longing, and then back at me, winked at me in this paternal way. "But hey. If camping isn't up your alley, you could try exercising."

I sat across from him with a 41-inch chest and a 30-inch waist. I had roughly 16-inch biceps, and he had the audacity to ask, "Have you tried exercising?"

If I hadn't been so let down, I'd have probably punched him.

One thing, though, I want to make abundantly clear: He was a good, kind, hardworking man. He was literally running a congregation with close to two hundred church members for zero money and on donated time, because he felt it was the right thing to do. He helped Mel and me move into our place. He called me when my son was born and gave me the warmest wishes. The problem wasn't with who he was as a human or as a man of God. The problem was with his misunderstanding that mental illness isn't a legitimate illness.

This is one of the most frustrating parts of living with mental illness. We'd never tell someone suffering from diabetes, "It's sad the way you take medication every day to feel normal," or, "Do you really need to see a doctor all the time to manage your illness?" or, "You could get over your diabetes if you just spent more time in the woods and kept yourself hydrated," or, "Have you tried exercising?" There's as much shame in having depression, anxiety, or any mental illness as there is in having heart disease, arthritis, asthma, or any other chronic illness.

It's hard enough living with mental illness. Trying to understand your own condition is even harder. But trying to navigate the way the world refuses to legitimize it as a chronic ailment, well my friends, that is just one huge slap in the face.

In that moment, though, I felt at odds with the world around me and at odds with the feelings I couldn't control. Every inch of this man, every part of him—the way his hands were open, the way he looked me in the eyes—said that he wanted to help. But his advice was nothing more than a result of decades of misunderstanding mental illness, and every word he said felt like a punch to the gut.

And to be real, I should have stood up for myself. I should have been more insistent and fought with him, but I was embarrassed. What he was saying made me feel like I should have been strong enough to handle the way I was feeling, and all of that made me feel ashamed for even asking for help.

Eventually, after we'd been sitting in his office quietly for an awkward amount of time, he took a long breath and said, "I suppose I could give you a blessing of comfort."

And I know, I know, those of you reading this from outside the Mormon faith are probably like,

"Potato-pahtahto." But a blessing of comfort was not a blessing for the sick. I won't go into the minutia of explaining the difference, because this book is about mental illness, not Mormonism. But you need to realize that a blessing for the sick uses two priesthood members and consecrated oil, while the other doesn't, and in this moment, it felt like a way to placate me after I'd twisted his arm for help.

It felt like I'd come to a doctor's office with a massive head wound gushing blood and was given a Band-Aid and the instruction to walk it off.

I remember leaving the bishop's office feeling completely helpless, kicking myself for discussing this problem at all—like even God couldn't help me. I felt embarrassed, and I felt like I was making a big deal out of nothing, when the reality was that I was completely miserable and considering suicide.

I think every single person suffering with mental illness has had between one and a million moments when they've confided in someone about how they were feeling, and they were met with criticism, misunderstanding, or straight-up scorn. And when I think about that, I realize that it's most likely the reason my mother held so firmly to her code of silence.

Ultimately, this moment caused me to bury my feelings even further. I continued hiding all of it from everyone, especially Mel. Openly discussing how I was feeling translated to embarrassment, and shame, and being treated like a child bawling over a scuffed knee. But as I look back now on those early days of our marriage, one thing is for sure: I should have been more open with Mel about what I was living with. And the longer I hid it, the more it felt like a grand lie that I should have confessed to her from the beginning.

"WHAT ARE YOU AFRAID OF?"

I was in the final year of a three-year MFA program for creative writing. I'd been off daily depression and anxiety medication for about seven years. Mel and I had two children now, Tristan and Norah, and the stress of raising a family while teaching classes and attending graduate school pushed my feelings of inadequacy to a level that felt a lot like absolute terror.

It was remarkable. I was getting straight As in grad school and publishing work in the same literary journals as my professors, and yet I felt like I was falling into a hole every day. I was one year from graduation, and the thought of finishing graduate school felt like I was on the *Titanic*—sure, there was a wonderful love story playing out, but this boat was not going to reach its destination.

I undercut all my achievements constantly.

Every single one.

If I got an A on a paper, I'd think about how I got a rejection from a literary journal. If I had an essay accepted for a publication, I'd think about how I had a bad writing day. If Mel called me a great dad, I'd kick myself over our most recent argument. My ability to sink something positive in my life by searching for something negative was a real work of art. It was like each day I set to work, using failure as my medium, to create my *Mona Lisa*: a life of insecure misery.

I used failure as my reason to get up in the morning. I actually told myself that if I didn't get up, I was failing. Each and every morning I said that to myself, and according to most therapists that isn't a good way to start the day. It's kind of like waking up to poison instead of coffee. Not that I drink coffee—because of the Mormon thing—but you get the idea.

It didn't take much to push me into a spiral of self-induced feelings of failure. And I use the term *self-induced* because part of me knew what I was doing to myself. I knew that I was the source of my own feelings of inadequacy, and yet I couldn't seem to stop myself from feeling like a huge failure. It felt like my brain just wouldn't allow me to think positively, like feelings of insecurity and focusing on the negative were as strong as gravity. And despite that I could logically see the good things in my life—my wife, my children, my successes in school and writing—they were never enough.

One day I forgot my lunch and I called myself a failure for a good 40 minutes because we couldn't afford the expense of my buying lunch. I finally ended up bingeing on fried chicken and waffle fries in the school quad.

I once burned my daughter's toast and hid in the bathroom, near tears, because I'd failed at something so simple.

And if real failure happened, oh wow! Watch out, my friends. During my second year of grad school, I flat-out failed the first section of my comprehensive exam. I was told that I'd have to retake that section. I got so anxious and so filled with dread that I broke out with hives for a week.

My decision to get a master of fine arts in creative writing didn't help with my feelings of inadequacy. The moment I told anyone about my choice of study, the response was, "What are you going to do with that?" I got so tired of the question that I simply began responding with, "Die broke and alone." I answered this way because it seemed like that's what people were already thinking, but after saying it so many times, I started to believe it myself.

And I know you are thinking, *If you were afraid of not making a living, Clint, then why did you decide to get an advanced degree in creative writing?* Well, that's a good question, and I'm glad you asked. The answer is complicated. Part of the reason was that I still labored under the notion that all you really needed was a degree to get a job—it didn't matter what the degree was. But mostly, I chose the MFA because writing was the only thing I ever felt good at, and that feeling alone was such a light in my otherwise dark self-esteem that I couldn't seem to give it up. I was kind of addicted to writing. I still am. So I just went for it, thinking that graduation was a long way away, and I wouldn't have to worry about any of that for a while.

But suddenly, graduation was only a year away. And let me tell you something about getting a master's degree in creative writing. It's awesome. It's a great time to just focus on writing and be around a lot of people who really love writing. But when it comes to simple, basic skills, like how to apply for a job or market yourself as a functioning human in the workforce, well, unless the employer is looking for someone to workshop a short story or provide a form-and-technique analysis of the most recent National Book Awards winner, you're out of luck.

The only job that I felt qualified to do was teach, and most of the jobs that paid enough to support a family required several years of adjunct teaching experience and a published book. As a grad student, I had maybe one year of teaching experience, and I was nowhere near close to being able to publish a book. When I thought about how unmarketable I was, I worried that I was going to finish school jobless and with a bunch of debt, and that felt like I was one year away from becoming my dad, who did in fact die broke and alone.

That realization ushered in complete and total terror.

Please keep in mind, I had this awesome family. Tristan and Norah were these adorable, charming, ever growing and changing treasures. I had a wonderful wife, whom I loved and admired.

I was feeling pretty comfortable in my role as a father. I couldn't think of spending time away from my children. I found four-year-old Tristan to be so interesting. I loved talking to him. Reading to him. Engaging with him. Each night, I'd lay in his bed, both of us side by side, a light near our feet that projected stars onto the ceiling. We'd play a game we called What Do You See Shaped like Stars? We called out our own constellations until we both fell asleep in his bed. I couldn't think of a better way to end my day. And Norah. Wow! I smiled whenever she came into the room on her rapidly moving, chubby two-year-old legs. She loved to lay me down on the ground, put blankets over me, and tuck me in for a nap, and each time she did, my heart melted. I looked forward to my time with her, and I was so interested in who she might one day become.

And all of that love for my family, that investment in who they were, caused me to feel even more like a failure, because when I thought about how wonderful they all were, all I could think about was how I needed to support them. And although I was excelling in my choice of study, it seemed impossible for me to make a decent living.

I'd been published in ten or so literary journals, and one of them once gave me fifty dollars. The rest didn't pay at all. I wasn't into math, or numbers, or Excel, but it seemed clear that being broke and alone was quickly becoming a very real option when I looked at my writing income.

I'd become a good dad and husband. Those fears of not being there for my family were gone, and they'd been replaced with my new fear that I'd never be able to provide for my wife and children.

Looking back on this time now, almost ten years later, I realize I absolutely had marketable skills, particularly when I take into account the graduate assistantship I held with the college of education during my first couple years in graduate school. But I was so frozen with self-doubt, and I'd convinced myself that there was only one road to survival: teaching, which seemed unachievable. All I could focus on was hopelessness, and I waited for something bad to happen, like it did so many times when I was child.

My anxiety prevented me from seeing the positive and realizing that I could find a way in this life, which I eventually did. I accepted a full-time student services job at a university in Oregon months before graduation. But living with anxiety during a challenging time, particularly during a time of impending change, made it almost impossible for me to see my own potential. I couldn't see that my future wasn't dark or dismal but full of possibilities. I couldn't see past the fog of anxiety. I couldn't see the blue sky because of the clouds. I couldn't seem to muster the strength to realize that there could be a sunrise at the end of a particularly dark night. I could go on with my metaphors, but essentially, I'd buried my head in the sand of my fear of failure, and this mindset was beginning to destroy my marriage.

To say Mel was sick of hearing about my fear of failure is an understatement. For several years, she tried to talk me out of it, reminding me that I was a good father and that I was doing well in school. She told me she loved me. She said that a lot. And naturally, I said it back to her. I absolutely loved her. But I got the impression that she felt like her love for me should be enough to pull me out of this funk. I think she wanted to believe that she made me happy, and the fact that I was so down on myself all the time contradicted that assumption.

And she did make me happy. She was a light in my life, and I couldn't imagine spending my life without her. But what I realized during this time was that I could have someone in my life that I really, honestly loved and valued and never wanted to lose. I could feel the warmth of love in my heart just looking at Mel and still have all those wonderful feelings overshadowed by dread and overwhelming feelings of failure. As much as I wished my love and admiration for my wife would overshadow my mental illness, sadly, that's not how it worked. I was slowly realizing that fact, and I think Mel was too.

Eventually, Mel just stopped engaging with my negativity, same as she did when one of our children wouldn't stop saying please after she'd told them no.

It all came to a head one evening. I was freaking out because I'd gotten two rejections from literary journals in one day, something that seems ridiculous now considering the few journals I was published in during this time were probably read by three people: the editor, the managing editor, and me. I mean, honestly, when's the last time you read a literary journal?

The kids were in bed for the night, and I was speaking in fast, incomplete sentences, half mumbling, half yelling, calling myself a failure, tears pooling in my eyes, face red, sweat dripping along my back. My right hand was shaking the way it used to, and I paced in the kitchen like a madman. I realize now that the way my shoulders slumped, the way I shook, the watery eyes, all of it was exactly the how my mother looked during her particularly down times in the months after my father left.

Mel approached me to ask what was wrong, and I said, "Don't. Just don't argue with me, okay? Just don't. I'm a failure. I'm a mess. I'm pathetic. You can say it, because it's true."

My mental illness was right there in front of her. Everything I was living with was on the surface now. I couldn't hide it anymore. The drywall, the flooring, the trim, all of it had been stripped away, leaving only rotting wood.

And rather than say nothing, and rather than argue with me about the way I was speaking about myself, Mel said something I'll never forget: "I can't do this anymore. I just can't. I love you, but I can't be the only one who loves you."

She paused for a moment. She was in gray pajama pants and an old blue university T-shirt, her brown hair pulled back. She looked at the ground and finally said, "You need to love yourself."

I looked at her blankly, unsure where I could

find something like self-love. It was a concept I'd never considered. At the time, self-love sounded as foreign as breathing underwater, or swimming to Antarctica, or flying out the second-story window of our townhome.

We looked at each other for a while, both of us knowing that something needed to change but not knowing what the next step was.

Finally I said, "I'm just so afraid. I'm always afraid. I think I've always been afraid, and I don't know how to make it stop."

Mel thought for a moment and finally asked, "What are you afraid of?"

And I didn't know how to answer her.

I was afraid of my past, and I was afraid of my future. I was afraid of my action and my inaction. I was afraid of who I was, and I was afraid that I could never become who I wanted to be. Yet if someone asked me who I wanted to become, I knew I couldn't define it. I was afraid to fall backward instead of forward, and yet moving forward sounded scary too. None of this made any sense, even to me, but it all felt real and terrifying, and I had no idea how to explain it to Mel, so I simply said, "Everything. I'm afraid of everything."

Mel ran her hand across her face, her blue-green eyes fixed on me as I stood in the kitchen, leaning against the counter, my legs trembling.

It was quiet for a moment. Then she said, "You have to do something. You have to go to the doctor about this. I can't do it anymore. You need to be on medication."

It seemed very clear that she was giving me an ultimatum. I needed to go back on medication, because our marriage was in jeopardy. And sure, we'd discussed that I was on medication for depression and anxiety before our marriage. But I'd told her that I didn't want to take it anymore, because medication, doctors, all of it reminded me of my father. Overall, she'd been supportive of that decision. At times, she even encouraged me to live drug-free because it seemed to her, like it did to me, that living that way meant I was in control of my anxiety. But as I had more and more moments like the one we were having, she'd begun to suggest that I might want to give medication another shot, saying things like, "Have you thought about going back on medication?" Or she'd ask me, after I'd visit the doctor, if I'd "asked what medications are available now for anxiety." But in this moment, she was direct, and I was left to decide between seeking professional help and jeopardizing my marriage—and as hard as it was to admit this at the time, it was probably the best thing anyone has ever done for me.

We went to bed after that, our backs to each other.

The next day, I called our family doctor and made an appointment to discuss my mental health and to restart the daily SSRI medication for depression and anxiety I was on before Mel and I got married. And without realizing it, I'd just taken

the first step in the hard work of learning to live a
healthy and balanced life with mental illness.

PART 4

FINDING
BALANCE

☺

I MAY NEVER BE HAPPY

I was driving through Minneapolis with a friend from graduate school. It was early November 2014. It was evening, with a windchill below zero, but not much snow was on the ground yet. We were going to dinner. I'd been out of graduate school for a couple of years, and I was now working in Oregon at a state university, in a program that supported low-income and first-generation students. It was work that I believed in and found very satisfying.

I was in Minnesota attending a professional conference. Jill was driving. She was a dear friend, a kind woman, who now wrote grants for a nonprofit. She mentioned how I'd been published in some bigger publications, like the *New York Times*. I'd been on *Good Morning America* after an article I wrote for the *Washington Post* went viral. She asked what that was like, and I told her it was terrible, an assessment I stand by to this day, and we both laughed.

"A cameraman actually came to my house, and he was there for at least five hours. Although it might have been more or less time, I'm not completely sure. I was so freaking anxious the whole time. It felt like they were there for twenty hours, or perhaps eternity, and it was everything I could do to keep from having an anxious puke fit on camera," I said. "I had only a few hours' notice before they came, and I cleaned like a maniac before his arrival, which was ironic considering the article was about my messy house. I ended up on the show for maybe five minutes, and all of it was terrible for my anxiety."

We discussed how I'd gained a decent online following. A year after finishing my graduate program, I'd started a daddy blog. At the time I started the blog, Mel and I were living in a cramped, stuffy, three-bedroom, third-floor apartment across from the fairground. I wrote that viral post about our messy home in the McDonald's PlayPlace at 5:00 a.m., because it was the only place I could go to get away from my kids so I could write. They also had free refills on Diet Coke, and that sort of thing really helps when you are writing at five o'clock in the morning after being up with a toddler. Around this time, I probably had twenty thousand Facebook followers. I'd eventually go on to have many more.

All in all, in the two years since graduation, things had worked out. I'd landed a good job with benefits and retirement, and Mel and I had recently bought our first home, a small thousand-square-foot, three-bedroom starter in a rural part of Oregon. Mel had decided to go back to school, and I was now supporting her education the way she supported mine. We had three children, and they were the sweetest people. I had a good marriage, and on paper, all those fears that I'd never be able to support my family because of my choice of study and that I'd never be a dependable father and husband because of my mental illness never materialized.

Just before we made it to the restaurant, Jill said, "You must be happy. It seems like things are really working out for you." And suddenly I had a harsh reality check. I wasn't happy. I had many good things in my life, and I'd overcome a pretty difficult childhood. I'd broken the cycle, finished college, and become, as far as I could tell, a decent and dependable father. I was still an active member in my church, and I'd had some success in writing.

And yet I wasn't happy.

I knew this in my core. I still struggled with bouts of anxiety and fear of failure. I was kind of waiting to get fired, but according to my most recent professional review I was doing a great job. I still undercut my accomplishments. Every single day. I was still taking an SSRI for anxiety and depression.

I wasn't meeting with a therapist.

And sure, I'd had happy moments. A lot of them, actually. But long-lasting, satisfied happiness free from anxiety and perpetual fear? I didn't know if I was capable of that. My default setting seemed to be feelings of failure and anxiety, and although my life situation had continued to improve, its impact on my mental health hadn't improved at the same rate.

I tried to explain this to Jill. We were pretty close in graduate school, and I confided in her about my mental health. But as I spoke, she just looked at the road and shook her head, unsure what to make of my assessment. From her view, everything was working out, and you know what? She was right. Everything was working out. But just because things were working out didn't necessarily equate to happiness. At least not for me, a man with mental illness.

Eventually, Jill went ahead and changed the subject.

But this moment of admitting to Jill, and ultimately to myself, that everything was going well and yet I was still scared of the future and pretty depressed and not capable of long-term happiness, well, it was significant. I'll tell you why: I'd somehow, on my own, admitted to one of the hardest truths of mental illness. It's a reality that doesn't make logical sense, and yet it's true.

Let me explain.

I had a loving, stable, and safe home. I had a good job and a good marriage. I had great kids. I'd defied the odds and overcome a troubled childhood. I'd broken the cycle and graduated from college, and yet I still struggled with long-term happiness. And as I tried to explain that to someone, I came across as ungrateful, and mopey, and in need of a reality check. Some of you reading this right now might be feeling the exact same way about me, and I get that. When I tried to explain this to myself, I thought, *You're mopey and you need a reality check, Clint.* And that line of thinking only fed the depression.

What I realized in this moment was that expecting myself to just get over my mental illness because my life had gotten better was like asking someone with diabetes to stop complaining and eat the chocolate cake they were given. Just because my life was getting better didn't mean that my mental illness had been cured.

It doesn't work that way.

But as we drove and I thought about this hard reality, I started to accept that this was my lot in life. My mental illness would not change or go away, and I was going to have to accept that fact. It was kind of like I was born without a leg. I'd spent most of my life trying to pretend that I had two legs, when the reality was my leg was gone and it wasn't coming back.

I needed to learn to live with one leg.

I had to accept that mental illness was part of me. I needed to accept that it was not going to just leave, regardless of my life situation. I couldn't wish it away or even pray that it would be taken from me. I couldn't hate it into submission or pretend it wasn't there.

This was the moment when I realized I had to learn to live a healthy and happy life with mental illness.

EMBARRASSMENT LOOKS A LOT LIKE AN EMOTIONAL BREAKDOWN

I couldn't think anymore. I mean, don't get me wrong, there were thoughts in my head, but they weren't adding up the way they should. I was sweating, and my vision was obscured by wacky shooting-star lines, and I couldn't for the life of me stop my hands from shaking. My grandmother often used the phrase *I can't think straight* for everything from traffic jams to bad gas. "Oh, honey! I've got the gas, and I just can't think straight. Ask me about that tomorrow."

But when your mind begins to swell with stress and anxiety until it truly doesn't work the way it used to, it's terrifying. It felt like these fearful emotions I was struggling with had crawled into my brain, and there just wasn't enough room for logic, and reason, and joy, and happiness, and rational thought, so part of my brain was pushed out my ears or my eyes or some other orifice to make room for the anxiety. My brain was jammed full of crazy half thoughts that I whispered to myself as I sat in my office sweating, slightly dizzy, with an anxious nausea in my gut.

I was experiencing a nervous breakdown, and it felt a lot like the surge of confusion and heightened senses I might have felt as a child with money in my pocket at a toy store. But it wasn't a good, carefree feeling of elation and confidence. It was the polar opposite of that feeling, like the weight of my life, the world, all of it was sitting on my chest. And although there was clearly air in the room, I couldn't seem to find enough of it.

Of course, this all happened at work, and right on cue, my director came into my office. I'm not sure what she wanted to discuss, but I can only imagine what she thought of me the moment I opened my mouth. She was a graying, curly haired, kindhearted woman with a PhD in literature, a dorky sense of humor, and an affinity for black sweatpants, white New Balance sneakers, and athletic polos. I tried to talk to her, but the words came out all jumbled, and I couldn't seem to form a single coherent sentence.

She kept asking me what was wrong, and I kept saying I didn't know. Only it didn't come out that cleanly. It sounded more like "Don't know . . . I . . . not sure. Can't. Just can't"—or some other Yoda-like ranting of a madman. When I think back on the way I was speaking, it sounded pretty similar to the way my father spoke to me in the parking lot of my wrestling match when he was high on painkillers. "You're gonna do real . . . Really. Pretty okay. Just really okay."

Once I accepted that my mouth wasn't lining up with my brain, I put my head down, and tried to hide the fact that I was on the verge of tears.

She suggested I go home, take a shower, and relax a little. Then she stepped out of my office, and I could see her standing next to my office door through the window for some time. I assumed she was trying to decide if she needed to send me to a psychiatric hospital. Or maybe she wasn't thinking like that, but *I* was thinking like that. I was wondering if I needed to have myself committed. I wondered if it was finally happening, and whatever had been coming loose in my brain had finally broken.

I was about a year and a half into a new job at the same university. I was working in the athletics department now, a job that I found somewhat ironic considering I once gave an argumentative speech in a communications class on why sports should not be part of college. I took the job because it was a step up in pay and responsibility and because my previous job was on a five-year grant, and it seemed like that program's funding could dry up at any moment. But what I didn't realize walking into Division I athletics, when I had zero experience working with college athletes, is that everyone— from the staff, to the coaches, to the students—were always, every day, on edge. These were the most high-strung people I'd ever encountered.

And they yelled a lot.

Particularly the coaches.

It was like their standard voice was five or six decibels above normal speaking.

For people that dressed like they were headed to a track meet every day, wearing athletic apparel with elastic waists and comfortable sneakers, all of it pretty casual, the stress of the department and the expectation to perform at 150 percent (a physically unachievable work percentage that was used pretty regularly around the office) weren't ideal for a man like me, living with an anxiety disorder.

In that first year, I built and redesigned a number of programs, and all of them went on to be successful—but the stress, the long hours, and the constant criticism that ultimately is the lifeblood of college athletics pushed me until I was sitting in my office, having a straight-up nervous breakdown and my boss was looking me in the eyes and kindly saying, "Go home. Take some time. Take a shower and calm down."

I cannot fully describe the foul-tasting embarrassment of being sent home because you had a nervous breakdown. I was in my midthirties, probably close to the same age as my father was when he began abusing prescription pills, and I recalled the long hours he spent in that shop behind our house, trying to run a business, and I wondered if he had a moment like this and if it was what pushed him over the edge and into addiction. And once again, those old fears of becoming my father sat in my lap, and then they went across my body in hot waves of nausea, all of it causing me to think more and more about how awesome it would be to take a few Xanax, or maybe a handful of painkillers, to just turn it all off and forget this ever happened.

Mel decided to go back to school during my last year of graduate school, which was awesome. I'd wanted her to do it for some time, but it wasn't until then that she felt ready. She was finishing up her four-year degree, and I was scheduled to watch the kids after work so she could study. She'd just got done with classes, and after picking up our three kids from school and daycare, she came home to find me in bed, in the middle of the day, curled in a ball.

She asked what was wrong, and I asked her to hold me. She crawled into bed, put her arms around my body, and I lay there feeling worthless. She asked what was wrong, and I said, "I can't. I just can't anymore."

Finally, I told her what happened at work. I told her my boss had sent me home, and how terrified I was that it was happening, that it was all crashing down and I was failing, and it was just a matter of time before I'd be fired because I wasn't mentally stable enough to hold down a career.

Which was far from the truth. In hindsight, I was doing a very good job. Grades across sports were way up, and they were continuing to go up. The programs I'd created were coming along nicely, and I was still writing and growing an online audience. I'd gotten a staff writing job for one of the most visited parenting websites online, and I'd recently raised close to ten thousand dollars through Kickstarter to self-publish my first book. I was teaching writing classes online and at the university I was working for. I was supporting Mel as she finished school, same as she'd supported me as I finished my education.

We were making it all work and I'd had success, but I was also getting up at 5:00 a.m. to write, going to work at a stressful job, teaching evening classes a couple times per week, then rushing home to watch the kids so Mel could study. Mel was doing homework on the weekends, as I graded papers with one eye and watched kids with the other. I was working myself to death.

I was still taking a daily SSRI for anxiety and depression, but it obviously wasn't enough. After I told Mel about what happened at work, she said, "Have you thought about going back to a therapist?"

It wasn't an ultimatum this time. It was more of an olive branch. It was a kind and well-timed suggestion from a loving spouse who was concerned about her husband, who might be losing his mind. I thought about my last stint in therapy. I thought about how I saw therapists the same as I did doctors, even though they couldn't prescribe drugs. I thought about how doctors reminded me of my father. I also tried to figure out when the heck I would have time to meet with a therapist, and I didn't know how much our insurance would cover, and I knew we didn't really have the money for extra bills.

It's kind of silly, but I sat there, in the middle of a nervous breakdown, thinking about the work that would go into finding a therapist, paying for therapy, and actually attending therapy, and it only made me more anxious. I thought about how the therapist might want me to live my life differently, and that also felt like more work, and I was already overworked. My anxiety was literally talking me out of going into therapy, which is kind of a dick move on the part of my anxiety disorder—but to be real, I'd lived with that manipulative, double-speaking, dickface long enough to know that this sort of play was exactly on-brand.

But in the moment, as I turned and looked at this wonderfully supportive and kind woman I loved, and as I thought about our three children in the other room, I thought about how I was feeling, how overwhelmed I was, and how, if I broke apart inside—really, completely broke apart—that would mean my family might break too. And although I still wasn't capable of processing complete thoughts, the reality of my family and my role as a father came through pretty clearly, and for the first time I fully realized that my mental health was bigger than I was.

My wife and my children were depending on me.

It was time to try therapy again.

It was past time, actually.

So I called my insurance, figured out the details, and ended up with a therapist appointment in one week.

I began meeting with a short, curly haired

therapist with dark eyes. During those sessions, I learned something that isn't often discussed when it comes to anxiety: People often talk about how mental illness is a detriment, and in many ways it is. But anxiety sufferers in particular tend to be high-functioning people, almost too high functioning.

This isn't to say that we are all high functioning. Some people with anxiety simply can't do all the things. And that's okay. But I think a lot of people often assume that mental illness looks like a lack of motivation to do anything, like it's an excuse to call in sick and hang out in pajama pants and a stained, extra-large university T-shirt and eat tubs of ice cream while watching the *Back to the Future* trilogy—only to realize that the future in the second film is the year 2015, and that future is in the past now, so you just sit there quietly, almost like you attended your own funeral, because you somehow outlived the future of your own childhood, and yet somehow you're not already dead.

And listen, I've been there. I've done that. And yes, it was both an awesome and depressing way to spend seven hours.

But depression was only part of my problem, and a lot of those depressed feelings were a self-confidence issue, which is, according to my therapist, on the menu for anxiety sufferers. Apparently anxiety often leads to perfectionism, something I didn't think I had at all considering I saw myself as a lazy slob, maybe even a long-term failure, who made nothing but mistakes all the time and more or less sucked at most if not all of the things. But according to her, the fact that I saw myself that way, when I actually was not, only proved to her that I was a perfectionist. We argued about this for some time, her showing me examples of perfectionism she plucked from my life and me telling her how they were clearly examples of my sucking, until finally we agreed to disagree.

But what we did agree on was that anxiety was, without a doubt, a huge motivator.

To say the least.

If I wasn't writing, I'd get anxious. If I wasn't tinkering with some program at work, trying to make it better, I'd get anxious. If I received even a sliver of criticism, I'd get anxious and run at fixing the problem with this crazy, stupid-fast, DC's the Flash–like speed—well, if the Flash also had cold sweats and stomach cramps and made trips to the restroom, where he sat on the toilet and worked from his phone because he didn't want his anxiety-related diarrhea to mess with his productivity.

About a year into therapy, I sold my first book to a real, honest publisher, and that was a huge source of awesomeness and stress. I was also adjusting to the pressures of a challenging job and trying to be the best father I could be, and all of those things caused my anxiety to tell me that things with my work, my writing, my family, all of it would get better if I just worked harder. And every time things didn't work out the way I wanted them to, I worked even harder. It was the same logic I used when I was overexercising. If I had an anxiety attack, I just needed to work out more so I'd be more tired. If I felt anxious about anything in my life, I just needed to work more.

So I got up earlier, I stayed later. I wrote more, engaged more with my online audience, taught more classes, engaged more with my wife and kids. And it was the *more* that was crushing me inside. I was doing more around the clock, always moving, always doing, trying to become a success, and my primary motivation was a fear of failure and anxiety avoidance. It was a dance that so many anxiety sufferers deal with. I was trying to gain control of my life, both hands white-knuckled on the wheel at ten and two, when what I needed to be doing was striving for balance.

My therapist made suggestions on how to relax more: schedule time off once a week, engage in a hobby that wasn't related to work, engage in regular meditation and mindfulness. As she made these suggestions, I thought about my father. I was living his workaholic lifestyle, and realizing that made me wonder if he'd gotten caught up in the same web of working harder to get where he wanted to be and when his drive began to betray him emotionally, he turned to prescription drugs to keep going. That was the first time I began to wonder, really wonder, if my dad had also suffered from mental illness.

But we didn't discuss my family all that much in therapy. What we discussed was healthy living and how to live a more balanced life. We talked about ways to pull back, to not seek over control situations. I began to better understand how to breathe down low, from my abdomen, and make time for deep relaxation and meditation. We discussed ways to look at situations with logic rather than panic. To realize that these work challenges and life challenges were pretty normal and not an indicator that I was failing at life—they were just an indicator that life is full of challenges that I was capable of overcoming.

We talked a lot about those things. About how I had the skills to handle life and that I needed to accept that I did. To have confidence in myself and my ability to cope.

This simple logical realization was very refreshing. It was like I'd been recast in *Star Trek* from Captain Kirk, with all that overacting and dramatic screaming, to Spock, with his calm and logical lifestyle.

And wow, I just read that too. I used a *Star Trek* analogy in my own book, and I'm pretty sure that's a new level of nerd.

But hey, we will get past this.

Right?

Please don't stop reading. It's the only *Star Trek* reference.

I promise!

But to give you an idea as to how much of a hold my "do more" lifestyle had on me, the moment my therapist suggested ways to pull back, to relax more, to take time off, I felt this wave of anxiety. I was afraid that if I did pull back, if I somehow found the will to do less, that I would become lazy.

I would stop being so productive, and then I would begin to fail at life. And all of that was just my anxiety feeding on itself, like it always had, so we addressed that too.

During that first year of therapy, I began to understand that anxiety, at least for me, was always there, and those constant, always-present anxious feelings caused me to search for the cause of the anxiety. Something must be making me anxious, right? Well, in my case . . . no. The anxiety was just there, always. Sometimes it was better, sometimes it was worse, but it was never fully gone, and trying to answer the question of what was making me anxious was a huge source of my problem.

I'd assume that something happened, or that I did something wrong, or that maybe the anxiety was a sign that something bad was going to happen. I'd search for the source of the anxiety, and since there really wasn't any logical reasoning for the emotion, I'd associate it with something random, like not exercising enough, or the assumption that I was actually failing at life, or some other nonsense.

But the reality was this: The anxiety was just there, regardless of what was happening in my life.

This isn't to say that there weren't stressful times that caused me to get anxious. I think that's the case for everyone. But for the most part, I was just an anxious dude, and what I needed to do was say, "I'm feeling anxious," and not try to find a reason for the anxiety, because often there wasn't one.

The anxiety was just there, regardless of the good, bad, or ugly in my life.

One of the best things I did was to begin saying to myself, "Clint, your brain is malfunctioning." And that realization helped me stop trying to associate my anxiety with something happening in my life, because searching for the reason for the anxiety was what caused me to slide into old habits like overexercising, or being afraid of clocks, or freaking out at work, or any number of other irrational actions I'd been up to for the past decade or so.

But one of the best therapy sessions I ever had was one year in. We were still meeting weekly. I sat across from my therapist, in that small two-story house that had been converted into an office building, and told her that I had all these good things going on in my life—wonderful kids, a good job, a wife I loved, a book coming out—and yet I couldn't enjoy them. All I could do was zero in on some argument at work, or some vile comment on my blog page, or something that happened years ago, or bad things that might happen in the future but probably won't.

"I churn it in my head until I'm an anxious mess, unable to sleep, and I become miserable," I said. "Each night before bed, I pray to be able to enjoy my blessings."

My therapist sat in a gray lounge chair, a computer in her lap, taking notes as I spoke. She thought for a moment, and then she told me that this was all typical of my condition, which was something she said all the time. She often described my concerns and my anxiety as normal or typical or in line with my condition. At first, these descriptions bothered me. There was something about living with anxiety—the years of hiding it, fighting it, denying it, being unsure what to make of it, hating it—that caused me to feel like it must be something more than normal.

She once said that I obviously had obsessive-compulsive disorder years ago, but now I probably just suffered from general anxiety disorder. It seemed clear that she wanted me to feel proud of the fact that I'd downgraded. That I'd gotten better and not worse, and yet general anxiety disorder sounded so, well, general. It sounded so vanilla, so bland, while what I was living with felt so Flamin' Hot Cheetos. I wanted her to call it "Bear Eating Me Disorder" or "Anxiety Is Consuming My Life so I Might as Well Drive into Oncoming Traffic Disorder." I wanted a label that better fit how disruptive anxiety had been to my adult life.

But the more I thought about the words she used, words like *normal* and *expected*, well, they were words I'd never associated with my anxiety, and I'd never heard another person use those words when describing anxiety. Usually, when I opened up to someone about my mental illness, they used words like *wired* or *crazy* or *sucks*, and then they made recommendations like, "Have you tried just not being anxious, because that's pretty stupid that you can't just not be anxious?" To which I would reply in my head, *Have you tried not being a dick-turd?* But ultimately I only responded with, "Yeah."

I was so used to seeing my mental illness as something to hide or be ashamed of. I thought about that meeting with my bishop years earlier, when he said, "You can't go around telling people stuff like that," almost like I'd just told him about some great sin or some horrible action from my past. Or maybe something outlandishly embarrassing, like admitting to shaving my head and gluing the hair to my butt just to see what it might look like.

Not that I actually did that, just to be clear, but you get the idea.

I thought about how my mother refused to tell anyone about her mental illness, almost like she was secretly a werewolf and she didn't want people to know that when the full moon hit the sky, she'd be out feasting on summer camps. I understood her fear now.

While my therapist's language bothered me at first, eventually I started to find comfort in the realization that what I was dealing with was, in fact, normal. It was something that lots of people lived with, and there was a playbook of tips and tricks that could make living with anxiety manageable, and all of that made me feel a raw surge of hope. It made me feel like I wasn't broken but normal and what I was living with was something lots of people live with. Millions and millions of people, in fact. And that realization helped me accept that my anxiety was part of me and wasn't something to be ashamed of but something to learn to live with. And I think this healthy acceptance of my mental illness is what I was missing the first time I attempted therapy. I went at therapy trying to get rid of the anxiety, when what I needed to do was accept that the anxiety was part of me and learn to live with it rather than try to exercise it into submission.

In some ways, when it came to motivation, it felt like my anxiety had shaped my life in a positive way. Sure, I had to manage it. But it wasn't all bad, and it definitely wasn't something to be ashamed of.

The therapist thought about my earlier question. About how I wanted to enjoy my life, my family, but felt I couldn't, and she asked me this very simple question that changed my life: "What would your life be like if you enjoyed yourself more?"

And I know that some of you reading this, those of you without mental illness, might not understand the impact of this simple question, but please realize that I'd never once, in my decades of battling depression and anxiety, considered imagining how my life might look if I enjoyed myself more. That's how overwhelming something like mental illness is. Depression, anxiety, all of it is so consuming that it's almost impossible to imagine life without it, so the prospect was unfathomable.

I'd never considered it.

When she asked me that question, I kind of scoffed to myself, and I put it in the back of my mind until later that night, when I was sitting next to my three-year-old daughter, trying to get her to sleep. It was dark except for the glow of Aspen's special pink flashlight. She was on the bottom bunk, and she shined the light at the bottom of her sister's bed and giggled, and as she did, I started to think about that question.

I started to compile a list of everything I'd do differently if I enjoyed myself more. I'd enjoy my time with my children more, like the moments I was having right there with my daughter, her soft hands holding her favorite flashlight, her eyes curiously moving side to side, my heart warm and quiet and content. Just her giggle alone, when I really thought about it, melted my heart. It was one of the most wonderful sounds I'd ever heard.

I thought about how, if I enjoyed myself more, I'd leave arguments at work, along with stress and unfinished duties. I'd approach work situations with the assumption that I was a qualified professional and not an impostor. I'd feel proud of myself for finishing college and landing a good job despite being raised with a drug-addicted father. I'd love my wife more and allow myself to feel confident and comfortable in our relationship. I'd feel good about my accomplishments as a writer and stop comparing myself to others. I'd slow down and laugh along with my children, and I'd hold them a little longer, savoring the moment rather than worrying about getting to the next thing on my long list of things to accomplish—a list that would never, despite my best efforts, be fully finished.

I'd stop comparing myself to my parents and realize that although they made mistakes, I had overcome the challenges of my childhood and become a good father, husband, and provider, and that reality was something I could take personal pride in without fearing that I might, at any moment, fall back into the hardships of my youth.

I felt a rush of something that I couldn't define, but if I tried to put a name on it, it'd be a mixture of confidence and relief. I didn't know where all this would lead. I didn't know if I'd finally found a breakthrough, but what I did know was that I fell asleep sitting in my daughter's bed thinking about that question.

And I slept better than I had since that first night I moved in with my grandmother.

LET'S ADDRESS THAT CHILDHOOD TRAUMA, SHALL WE?

I was almost 30 years old before I heard the term *opioid epidemic*. I may have heard it on National Public Radio, but I'm not completely sure. I do remember not associating it with my father at first. I assumed it had to do mainly with heroin, and not the overprescribing of opioid painkillers. It took my hearing the term over and over again throughout the next several years before I started to pause and say, "I wonder if my dad was a victim of the opioid epidemic?"

It took me quite a while to sit down and make that assessment. Probably longer than it should have, and I think I needed to hear about the opioid epidemic at least a hundred times before I could accept that perhaps my dad was caught up in something that wasn't his fault. And I think the reason it took so long was because part of me knew that if I thought about Dad in this light, it would change the way I remembered our relationship.

My dad did some pretty crummy things to me and my family when he left. And it took my getting my own family and seeing how much I loved and admired my children, and particularly my wife, to finally become angry with him. I couldn't look at my own children and wife and imagine walking out on them like that, not to mention not paying child support while also brandishing my mistress in the backyard. But anger wasn't the only emotion. There was also the disappointment of never feeling a rich connection with my father, the heartache I felt watching him slowly die from drug addiction, and the fear I lived with for most of my young life that I might somehow follow in his footsteps.

And sure, he was dead and had been dead for years, and yet when I thought about him, I wanted to hang on to that bag of mixed and troubled emotions. I wasn't ready to try to find some new way to approach his memory, because that might lead to forgiveness. And I definitely wasn't ready to do that.

Not at all.

So I put blinders on for a while. When the opioid epidemic was discussed on the radio, I changed the station. When it came up on a TV show or the newscast, I changed the channel. When friends talked about it, I changed the subject.

But then, in early 2020, one of the publications I was writing for asked me to cover a show on Netflix called *The Pharmacist*. For me, the son of an opioid addict, that show was a punch in the gut, and yet I couldn't look away. It followed

the story of Dan Schneider in the late 1990s and
early 2000s as he caught his son's killer. His son's
death propelled him to start looking differently
at the OxyContin prescriptions coming from his
own pharmacy and led him to wonder if he was
becoming a killer himself.

My father died in December 2001. As someone
who lived the opioid epidemic, I felt many old
memories stirred up as I watched the four-episode
docuseries discuss things I had been too young
to understand but that I found very recognizable.
As far as I know, Dad never went to a pain clinic
like the one run by Dr. Cleggett in Dan Schneider's small town outside New Orleans. But surely
he could have. I remember occasionally going
with my father from one doctor to another. He'd
complain of pain and leave with multiple prescriptions. And then we'd go to multiple pharmacies to
get them filled.

The part of the documentary that really gave
me pause, however, was how many people—from
drug reps, to doctors, to other pharmacists—were
complacent in years of overprescribing addictive
opioids. The show interviewed a former Purdue
Pharma sales representative. In the fourth episode,
he mentioned that he wasn't dumb, and that the
people above him weren't dumb, and that the
doctors and pharmacists he was meeting with
clearly weren't dumb. They all knew what was going
on, and yet they played dumb. None of the people
pushing these drugs were oblivious, but they chose
to continue because of simple greed. According to

the *New York Times*, between 1995 and 2001, the time frame covered in *The Pharmacist* and the time frame of my father's addiction, OxyContin brought in $2.8 billion in revenue for Purdue Pharma. That is a bonkers amount of money, and obviously it was enough for many, many people to turn a blind eye as they prescribed it to addicts like my father.

But I'll tell you about the part of this show that caused me to wake up in the night and just stare at the ceiling, my mind racing. It was when experts featured on *The Pharmacist* started talking about the death rattle, the wet, gasping-for-air sound drug addicts make right before they die from an overdose.

I knew that sound.

It was the same sound I heard from my dad the day my brother and I found him overdosing in his pickup truck.

I finished that show, and I finally realized—*really* realized—that my dad was caught up in a dangerous sales pitch pushed by pharmaceutical manufac-turers that convinced doctors to complacently put patients on more and more pain medication.

Suddenly, for the first time, it felt like a light came on and I could better see my dad's story. I started to realize that maybe my father's drug addiction, all the hardships he placed on my mother and me—all the marriages, the time in jail, the legal problems, all of it—might have been part of something bigger than he was. I thought about those early surgeries he had. The ones that happened when I was so young, and I thought about all the pills he must have been prescribed, and I started to wonder if that turning point in his life I'd been trying to find, the one that would show me where he went wrong and how I could avoid his mistakes, happened before I could remember and happened in the hands of a trusted doctor.

It was around this time, when I was 37, that I started meeting with a new therapist. My old therapist left on maternity leave, so I was reassigned.

My new therapist was this skinny, kinda awkward, middle-aged, black-haired man with bloodshot eyes that, for the most part, were never completely open except for when he was going to make a point, and then—*bam!*—they'd open all the way, and it felt like he was looking at my soul. He had an affinity for pastel polo shirts that he unbuttoned just enough to let his clients, myself, God—everyone—know that he had this spackle of very dark curly chest hair.

But on the whole, he was bright, and thoughtful, and clever in a lot of ways. One of his best suggestions was that I should try laughing at my anxiety. He casually mentioned that I'm a funny guy, and he asked if I ever thought about making fun of those anxious feelings.

"Have you ever tried mocking them?" he asked. He went on, suggesting that I laugh at the anxiety, the same way I do at myself, with my trusted brand of self-deprecating humor. It was a genius idea. It felt like I'd brought this big, snarling, sharp-fanged, hairy monster that had tormented me most of my life into the room and made fun of its tiny nipples.

But his real contribution to my mental health journey was during the COVID-19 pandemic. I was meeting with him online in my closet, because it was the only place in my house where I could get away from my children. There was something about 2020 that made me long for my children to finally get that letter from Hogwarts informing them that they'd been accepted to wizarding school, so that I could send them off to learn magic and have amazing adventures and I could stop making 800 meals a day because magic would feed them.

Or house elves.

Or whatever.

My point being, I felt like my family was on top of me all the time, and finding somewhere to sit and chat about my mental health seemed impossible, so I hid in a closet, the lights low, all of it feeling like I was doing something naughty—or hiding from a murderer.

My therapist started asking me questions about my parents, and I couldn't avoid telling him about my father and the way he dramatically left my mother and then built a fence between his end of the yard and hers in some *I Love Lucy*-style expression of dominance. I told him about the drug addiction, and I mentioned watching *The Pharmacist*.

Suddenly, we were addressing my childhood trauma, something I'd intentionally avoided with my other therapists. I told my first therapist I couldn't remember much from my childhood. Which was a total lie. I probably remembered it better during those earlier sessions than I do now, but to be real, I was pretty young at the time, only eighteen years old. My father was still alive and addicted, and my mother and I were still not speaking. I really didn't know how to address those issues as they were happening. I'm not going to say that he never asked about it—he did. But he didn't push it.

My second therapist never brought it up.

But this guy, he went right to the heart of it. We discussed the foundations of my anxiety, the beginning of it all. And he gave me this very simple explanation: "Some people are born with a proclivity toward mental illness. It's just in their DNA. And some people are nurtured into it. Perhaps a tragic experience or childhood trauma caused them to develop an anxiety disorder. Some people really hit the jackpot, and they get both. I think you are one of those lucky people."

It was a depressing stroke of luck.

But as I told my therapist about my parents, he asked if my dad had ever been diagnosed with bipolar disorder.

"Oh, wow. No," I said. "There's no way. No. I don't think so. I mean, I know he'd never have gone to a therapist. He was . . ." I paused for a moment, trying to find the right words. I wanted to say "too masculine" at first, because that really was how he'd have described himself. He was a work-with-your-hands, wear-Wrangler-jeans-and-leather-boots kind of guy. He wasn't really into self-care, or mental health management, or admitting that he occasionally went on long drug binges that caused him to swerve his pickup across yellow lines, only to get pulled over and then flatly call the police officer "a no-good fuzz dick."

"His way of fixing things was to work through the pain," I said. "Maybe put a little dirt on it." Finally, after a long pause, I said, "My dad was a cowboy. A tough guy." I made pistols with my hands, and said, "Pew-pew."

The therapist laughed and said, "Just hear me out, okay?" Then he went on to say that the story I was telling, he'd heard it before. It was a common story from the '90s and 2000's: Someone with undiagnosed bipolar disorder gets prescribed opioids. They get addicted to them under the oversight of a doctor. "Then when they go into a manic state," he said, "the opioids make the mania ten times as bad. Maybe a hundred times. Worse than it's ever been. They feel better than you or I could even imagine. And then they do some crazy, impulsive, manic things, like having an affair and then hiring that woman to work with them in the backyard."

As he spoke, I felt like I'd been hit with a truck.

He went on, "Then, when the mania stops and they get really depressed, they turn to opioids to numb themselves because of the depression. But that only makes the depression worse. However, they're addicted now, so they can't really stop."

It was quiet for a moment.

My mind was racing.

Finally he asked, "Does this sound familiar to you at all?"

As he asked the question, I thought back to this moment, when I was sixteen, and I stopped by unannounced to check on Dad. It was just before he went into jail for 180 days. He'd separated from his most recent wife, and he was living in this one-bedroom ramshackle blue house with a very long black driveway, not far from my grandmother's home. I knocked on the door, and he didn't answer; however, I could see him sitting on the living room floor through the window. The door was unlocked, so I went in. Dad was in nothing but faded navy blue boxer briefs, with a phone book in his lap, a corded telephone upside down and against his ear. His skin was pale, his neck, forearms, and face the color of stained oak from working in the Utah sun and slathered with freckles. The phone had been off the cradle for some time, so it was beeping. He looked up at me with tears in his eyes, pupils open wide and dark black. He started mumbling something and pointing at the phone book, but none of it made any sense.

I took his arm, pulled him to his feet, and walked him into the bedroom. His mattress sat on the floor, the bedding tan and brown and wadded up at the foot of the mattress, white sheets stained, cardboard boxes lining the wall on the far side of the room, pill bottles strewn across the windowsill, and half a bottle of brown liquor within arm's reach of the bed. I tucked him in, and I closed the bedroom door. After a few moments, he started crying in the bedroom, but when I went back in, he waved his arm in a shooing motion that told me to leave. So I just sat in the living room, until I was sure he was asleep.

I hadn't thought about this moment for years, but I knew now that this was one of his down times. And as I thought about that moment, it felt like more lights had come on in my father's story. I could see in the shadows now, the dark places. I started to map it out. I thought about how he seemed so different when he left. How I didn't recognize him. I thought about how brazen he was in the backyard with his new girlfriend, the make-out sessions in his truck, and his overwhelming confidence. The way he spent money on credit just before he left my mother. I thought about all the times he declared bankruptcy.

Then I thought about the time he overdosed in his pickup. This must have been when the mania stopped. I thought about his time in jail, when he gave me that advice. He looked like he'd fallen in a hole and couldn't get out. Yes, he was in jail, and I assumed that was the reason. But now I assumed there was something more.

As I chatted with my therapist, I started to realize that maybe I was doing exactly what I should have been doing. I was doing what my father never did. What maybe he felt he couldn't do. I was accepting my mental illness for what it was, and I was working on learning to live with it.

Yes, I was taking more medications now, but I wasn't abusing them. I was using them with caution. And yes, I was meeting with a therapist and a psychiatrist, but I wasn't doctor shopping.

I was engaging in healthy habits like meditation, downtime, and healthy self-talk. I had some tips and tricks up my sleeve to make my life with mental illness sustainable. It wasn't cured, sure. It would probably never be completely gone, but I was accepting it as part of me and learning to live with it.

I guess what I'm trying to say is that I'd started to own my anxiety disorder in a way my parents, particularly my father, never did. And that realization alone made me feel more hopeful than I'd ever felt before.

We were nearing the end of the session, and I was still reeling from what he'd told me when he said, "I want you to imagine a younger version of yourself is standing before you, awkward and nervous, with buckteeth and greasy bleached hair parted down the middle, dressed in baggy '90s clothing."

Okay, he didn't tell me to add all those details, but I knew how I looked in the '90s.

Anyway, he asked me what I would tell my younger self if I had the chance.

All I could think about was when I was fifteen and I'd been living with my grandmother for a year or so. My father was a drug-addicted mess. My mother and I weren't speaking. I was terrified of both of them. Looking back now, it's hard to deny that my parents both suffered from mental illness, and yet they didn't understand how to manage it. I don't think they even would have had the options available to manage it, and if they did, they would probably would have felt like it wasn't socially acceptable to admit to having mental health concerns and to seek out help.

But I wasn't my parents.

I had other options.

One of my biggest fears as a teenager was that my grandmother, who was in her late seventies but appeared ancient, would die and I'd be forced to move back in with either my mother or father. I would sit up in bed at night, a pit in my gut, afraid. Sometimes, when the fear got to be too much, I would sneak into Grandma's room and place my finger under her nose to make sure she was still breathing.

In my closet, the therapist on my computer screen, I closed my eyes and thought of that awkward, scared young man I used to be. My therapist told me to think about what I knew now and about how my life had turned out. Then he told me to think about what I would tell my younger self if I had the chance.

I could see myself in my mind's eye, and I looked at that frightened, confused young man I used to be, and I told him that he didn't need to be scared anymore. "You're going to overcome all of this," I said. "Grandma is going to see you through high school. You will get married to a wonderful person. You will go to college, and have children, and get a good job, and own a house, and all this madness, this inconsistency, this fear you feel every day will get more manageable. You're going to be okay."

Then my younger self looked up at me and smiled, and I felt the warmth of knowing that I didn't have to be afraid anymore. It was a wonderful, freeing feeling that I hadn't known I needed but that I couldn't help but feel overwhelmingly grateful for.

UNPACKING
MY FATHER

After discussing Dad with my therapist, I stopped trying to avoid his memory and I started looking directly at it. The first step was getting a copy of his death certificate, and the official cause of death was listed as an idiopathic stroke, something I'd never heard of and didn't remember being discussed during the time of his death. So I called a doctor friend of mine—we'd known each other from church—and asked him a few questions. He told me something interesting. He said that sometimes, when someone has been dead for a few days, like my dad was, it's very difficult to determine a cause of death unless it's obvious, like a gunshot wound or a broken neck. But if the person had a drug addiction, and that's been documented, like it was with my father, a stroke is pretty common. Years of drug addiction can cause a stroke, sure, but then he said something that gave me pause: "Trying to get clean after years of drug addiction can also cause a stroke."

So I reached out to an attorney friend of mine, and he helped acquire a copy of my dad's criminal record. On a timeline, I mapped out the dates, the offenses, and the time in jail, along with what I knew of his marriages and other life events. Most of the offenses I knew about. Some were surprising. Sometimes I realized I had the dates wrong, and as a teen it felt like he'd been in jail much longer than 180 days. I even published a short essay in grad school that said he'd been in jail for 18 months, which was obviously inaccurate.

In the end, though, the last charge on his record was something I didn't expect. One year before his death, a few months before I graduated from high school in 2000, he was charged with a felony for driving with an open liquor container and a suspended license. Dad never told me about this, or at least, I don't remember it happening. I do remember hearing that he showed up to my high school graduation very intoxicated, and was screaming like he used to at my baseball games, saying, "That's my boy!" But he was asked to leave by some high school administrators before I saw him.

After his felony charge, he was placed on probation for one year as a way to avoid more jail time. The felony was dropped, but the document I found didn't list why. It also didn't list the details of his probation. I tried to get more details on all of this but unfortunately, according to the Utah Fourth District Court, records that old would have been destroyed. But according to my lawyer friend, it's very likely that he was mandated drug and alcohol counseling as part of that probation.

This would have included monitoring all the pills he took, providing urine samples, meeting with a drug and alcohol counselor, the works. It would have been a level of oversight he sorely needed.

And suddenly I thought back to that Mormon temple recommend I found while cleaning out his apartment. And I thought about something my half-brother said years later, as we were discussing our shared father's death. Scott and I don't talk all that much. Probably a few times a year. He's about eight years older than I am and was raised by his mother, my dad's first wife. I never lived with him, and our relationship has been spotty at best. There are moments when we've tried to be close, but then we drift apart for years, only to randomly call each other and catch up. But to be fair, most of my family is like this, and I think it has more to do with the fallout of drug addiction and multiple marriages than it does with who we are as people. One day, five or six years ago, we were chatting over the phone, and I said, "After Dad's overdose."

And he said, "Overdose? No. No, Dad was getting clean. That's what killed him."

At the time, I sat there, in silence, convinced that he had no idea what he was talking about. It was so obvious that Dad died from a drug overdose. I knew it. In my core I knew it, and I think part of me just wasn't ready to believe anything otherwise. I'd spent so many years being haunted by my dad's memory and the hardships and uncertainty he caused for me as a child: The fear of becoming him. The difficulty of watching my father slowly kill himself with drug addiction. The jail time. The tears and stress my grandmother and my mother suffered. All of it was so present and real and heartbreaking that I simply wasn't ready to change the story I knew. I must have said a million times, to a million people, that my dad had died of a drug overdose.

But now, as I read through this official court document telling me that Dad was on probation, and hearing that he most likely was mandated to participate in drug counseling, I was left to question that assumption. So I called my half-brother, Scott. I told him about what I'd found regarding Dad's death certificate, and his criminal record, and the probation, and I finally asked him. "Years ago, you said Dad was getting clean when he died. How did you know that?"

Scott was quiet for a moment. He reminded me of our father, from the slight rural Utah twang in his voice, to the work boots and tight jeans that he often wore, to the fact that he does heating and air-conditioning work professionally. Scott finally said flatly, "Because he told me he was." He went on about Dad's probation and how they monitored every pill, although he never mentioned exactly who "they" were, and I assumed he was referring to some sort of law enforcement. "He didn't have a lot of wiggle room near the end, so he kind of had to get clean. I don't think he liked it at first, but near the end, I think he was really trying. For me, that's the hardest part about how he went."

And once again, more lights came on in Dad's story, and suddenly I realized that my dad, at the end, was trying to become something else. I wished it would have happened many years earlier. Maybe he'd still be here to be a grandfather to my children.

Once I finished chatting with my brother, I thought about a conversation I'd had with my half-sister a few months before I talked with Scott. She mentioned that my nephew got a summer job at a heating and air-conditioning company. The owner of that company was an old friend of my dad's named Frank. Apparently, he pulled my nephew aside one day and told him that my dad, his adoptive grandfather, wasn't a bad man. At one time he was a very good person, and that many of those mistakes he made were the drugs, not him.

My nephew just shrugged, because he'd never even met my father. He died when my nephew was very young. I think my sister told me this story as a kind of funny anecdote. But it stuck with me for one very important reason: This was one of the only times I'd ever heard someone say anything nice about my father.

So I called Frank, and I asked him what he meant.

He was still running that same company in Utah County. The business had two locations, one in Utah County and another in southern Utah. According to Frank, he was "good and tired and getting ready to retire." He suggested that we meet next time I was in Utah. Then he asked, "My dad knew your father pretty well also. Do you mind if he meets with you too?"

I told him that would be amazing.

That summer I met Frank and his father, Sam, in a conference room of the company they'd built together. Frank was a slender man in his early sixties, with brown hair, a good tan from working in the Utah sun, and bright white teeth. His father was much older, with the same build, and a little less hair, and a hearing aid.

I told them that I'd never met anyone who had much good to say about my father, and Sam laughed. Then he leaned across the table, pointed at me, and said, "Well, son. That's going to change today."

Together they told me that they met my dad in the '80s, and my father trained them both to do residential heating and air-conditioning work. "Your father was one of the most skilled technicians I'd ever met," Frank said. "And I've been at this work for a lot of years now."

The three of them worked together on multiple jobs for many years but slowly drifted apart about the time my father left my mother. Frank was going through a divorce while my father was teaching him the trade, and my dad was his confidant.

"He really helped me through that struggle," he said.

Frank leaned back at one point, and said, "You know, there's a man I know that I taught to do heating and air-conditioning work about fifteen years ago. He now owns his own company, and every time we run into each other, he calls me his mentor. And when he does that, I smile and think about your dad, because he was my mentor. I wouldn't be where I am today without him. He was a good man before the drugs."

Sam nodded across from his son. Then he tapped the table to get my attention, and said, "A very good man. I've never met someone who worked harder and who cared more about what he did. I learned a lot from him, even though he was younger than me. It was a privilege to know him. He was a really good memory in my life."

As they spoke, I thought about my dad's business in the backyard and wondered if things had worked differently for my father and me, maybe our life might have looked a lot more like Frank's and Sam's, a father and son running a company together.

Several years earlier, just before I left for graduate school in Minnesota, my aunt delivered a flimsy corrugated box of old photos. She said they were photos of my father. I hadn't seen her for a few years, and I was surprised by how much she resembled my grandmother, petite with tight shoulders and gray curls. We spoke for a moment. She asked about my son and gave me some story-books for him.

I was home alone the day she visited. I sat on the floor, the soles of my feet touching, knees falling to the sides, and placed the box within the circle of my legs. At the time, I had only two photos of Dad. One was attached to his obituary, the faded black and white image showing a scrawny man with unkempt hair. The other was his driver's license that I acquired while cleaning his apartment after his death. Inside the box were two-by-two-inch slides to be used in an overhead projector, lined up neatly in Styrofoam sleeves. I held the first slide up to the living room light. It was small, distorted, and the light shining through the film gave the image an amber tint. I had to hold the cell close to my face to make it out.

I flipped through the slides and the years, watching Dad's face crack and his smile become short and flat. Weight evaporated from his body as his skin grew tough and stretched across his face, his drug addiction becoming more and more obvious.

For many years, these small slides were the only pictures I had of my father.

But then, around the time I spoke with Frank and Sam, I got a message from an old friend I grew up with. She'd been going through some old photos of her parents and found a picture of my brother and I, at the Fourth of July parade in Provo. We were on this big sheet-metal airplane that my dad had constructed for us to pedal along the parade route. I couldn't have been more than six years old.

Dad's face was shaven, and he wore a clean, tucked-in polo shirt and jeans. He looked focused, leaning over the plane, carrying a small gut. He was with my mother, and she was looking at him with admiration. I was smiling and pointing at something, wearing the most adorable aviator hat and goggles.

This was a side of my father I can only slightly recall in foggy memories that are so close to a dream I often question if they are real.

That photo felt like a piece of evidence of a former, drug-free Dad, so I looked closely, examining the pitch of his shoulders, the arc of his arms, the way the knees sagged in on his fallen arches. This was the father I'd always longed for, the past-tense Dad, the binary, the *good man* that his old friends Frank and Sam told me about.

And suddenly all the lights were on now, and I started to realize that in my own story, my life, I'd made Dad the villain.

In my narrative, Dad was a flat, evil character that I didn't understand and had no intention of ever giving the benefit of the doubt. But actually, he was a complex man who was a victim of his time and place. I'd been afraid of his example and afraid that I was going to become him. Later, I just became angry about his choices and the way he walked out. I looked at my own wife and children, and I couldn't understand how he could have done those things. I didn't understand how any man could.

But now, I was seeing the whole story for the first time, and it seemed so clear that my father was a hardworking dude who probably had undiagnosed mental illness but never sought help because that wasn't his style and it wasn't socially acceptable at the time. He fell into drug addiction during the early days of the opioid epidemic. It exacerbated his bipolar disorder, and sadly he became one of the opioid epidemic's earlier victims.

I was starting to understand that my dad was the kind of guy who would mentor someone else and help them through a rough patch in their life. The kind of dad who would build a pretty sweet handcrafted sheet-metal plane for his two sons to ride during a Fourth of July parade. The kind of man whose wife would look at him with total admiration.

Not a horrible man without redemption.

I knew my dad did some bad and hurtful things. He broke laws, he hurt my family, and he died far too young. None of this new knowledge justified his actions, but by better understanding who he was, and why, I found peace.

This is what I'd always been missing with my father's story. This juxtaposition. The past details that made him not some flat, evil drug addict but a real, honest human who was a product of an epidemic, a failed system, and a societal misunderstanding of mental illness that ultimately made him who he was and helped explain why he made the mistakes he did. And it seemed very likely that he was trying to find that redemption during the final months of his life, and that realization made his death all the more tragic.

While I still struggled to forgive him for some of his actions, I was also overcome with empathy for his situation. And that empathy felt a lot like forgiveness, and that forgiveness made me feel like the weight in my chest, the heaviness I'd been dragging around my whole life, was a lot lighter. And while adding up all this information had my mind spinning for several days, I couldn't stop myself from smiling in relief.

And suddenly I was hit with the very harsh realization that maybe all this time I thought I was afraid of becoming my father, but what I was really afraid of was myself. I was afraid that I couldn't live with my anxiety. But now that I'd done the hard work of finally understanding who I was, where I was from, and what I needed to do to live with my mental illness through therapy, medication, and lifestyle changes rather than try to control it, I realized that I had the tools I needed to live a happy life as a fully functioning father and husband, and I didn't need to be so afraid of myself anymore.

I didn't know if I'd ever felt so free.

EPILOGUE

THEIR INHERITANCE

I was driving home with my fourteen-year-old son, Tristan. It was a Saturday and his birthday, and we'd just picked up a gift from his best friend. He was in a blue hooded zip-up jersey jacket and black adidas track pants, his dark brown hair cut just above the shoulders. He looked so much like me at his age, from the blue-green eyes, to the braces, to the long hair—as we talked, I thought about how I was his age when I left my mother's home. Only he didn't have a lot of those stresses. For the most part, he had a pretty stable house, and yet I knew he'd been struggling with anxiety.

He showed me the gift. It was a stress-relieving handgrip. He mentioned that sometimes when he got anxious, he broke pencils, pens, small things, so his friend gave him a stress grip to help.

It was thoughtful, I will admit.

And then, as we drove, he opened up about his anxiety for the first time. He told me about stomach pains, cold sweats, trouble sleeping and concentrating, and how he just felt nervous sometimes.

So I reminded him that I have the same problem. I'd told him about it before, but he was a teenager, and—let's be real—I don't know if he'd ever really been all that interested in anything I've overcome.

But at this moment, he seemed to really be listening.

"When did you start getting it?" he asked.

I thought for a moment and said, "I was a little younger than you are now. But my dad was gone. He was struggling with drug addiction. And my mom was working two or three jobs to make ends meet. So she wasn't around all that much. I just had to manage it on my own. Not that I did a very good job of it."

"How did you make it go away?" he said.

I let out a breath.

"I didn't. I still have it. I always will. What I had to do was go to a therapist and learn how to accept it as part of me. I had to learn to live with it rather than try to find a way to live without it. If that makes sense."

"Oh," he said. It was quiet for a moment. He looked at the road as we drove, and I could see the realization that all anxiety sufferers get when they finally comprehend that it's never going away.

Then he said, "This sucks. It's my birthday. And I was anxious like all day, and I just don't understand. I don't like feeling this on my birthday."

He was looking out the window now, at a large forest of Oregon evergreens between his friend's home and ours, his right hand working the stress grip.

I looked over at him and said, "Yeah. Sorry, buddy, but that's not really how anxiety works."

I reminded him of his sister's ADHD. "Everyone gets distracted sometimes, but for people with ADHD, it's an all-the-time thing. They are almost always distracted. Being distracted, struggling to focus, it's the default, and it doesn't necessarily need a trigger."

He nodded, but continued looking out the window.

"So?" he asked in a very typical "What does this have to do with me?" teenager way.

"Anxiety is the same way," I said. "Everyone has anxious moments, but at least for me, and probably you too, the anxiety is kind of always there, even when things are going well. Just last Christmas I had a horrible anxiety attack, so I get it. Most of the time, it just happens without a trigger at all. But the part that sucks the most is how you'll think to yourself that something must be triggering it, so you start to associate the anxiety with irrational things, like organization, or not getting enough exercise or sleep, or the fear that something bad might happen even though it's unlikely. For me, that's when my anxiety turns into obsessive-compulsive disorder. But the anxiety is always there, regardless of good times or bad times."

I went on for a moment more. Eventually, I looked over at Tristan. He was still looking out the window, gripping his stress grip harder than before, and I wondered if I was doing more harm than good, but I also realized how much I wished I'd learned all of this at his age, rather than in my midthirties.

It was quiet for a moment, and finally I said, "It's not hopeless, buddy. I promise. Listen, I still hate it. But I know that it's part of me, and there are things I have to do to manage it. But as long as I do them, I'm pretty okay. Most days I don't even notice it."

He thought about what I said. It was quiet. Then he asked, "What do you have to do?"

I pointed at his stress grip.

"Things like that. I mean there's more, but that's a great place to start. But hey, I'm pretty similar to you in all this. I'll show you a few things. You know, different ways to breathe, for example. How to talk to yourself in a positive way. How to realize that it's the anxiety and not the situation. But on the positive side, do you know what happened when I learned to live with my anxiety instead of trying to find a way to get rid of it?"

"What?" he asked.

"Well, my life got better. I got happier. I started smiling more, and I stopped being so afraid all the time. And when I look back at my life thus far, I've gone to college. I've gotten married, gotten a good job, and had three amazing kids. All of it with my anxiety in the back seat. Life's been pretty good despite my anxiety. Pretty sure it's going to be the same for you."

I gave him one of those soft, fatherly punches to the arm. He let out this long breath, and I could almost see the steam of feeling odd or like he was holding on to some great burden alone come pouring out of him. Then he said something I think all dads never, ever, get tired of hearing.

"Thanks, Dad."

"Anytime, kiddo. Anytime."

EPILOGUE
PART 2

yOu'RE DOING IT

It was 2021, and Mel and I were at church for the first time in months because of the COVID-19 pandemic. All three of our kids sat together on a long church bench. Tristan was fourteen, with shaggy, long brown teenager hair, his white button-up shirt half untucked, doing his best to pay attention but not really paying attention. Norah, our eleven-year-old, was in an adorable purple and pink floral-print dress, hair perfectly combed, wearing her brown-framed glasses and white flats. Aspen, our seven-year-old caboose, was looking around the chapel, eyes ever curious, brown bangs in her eyes, hair getting more and more tangled with each wiggle on the bench, wearing a dress that matched her older sister's.

The kids were sandwiched between us, me in a blue dress shirt, black slacks, and black tie, Mel in an absolutely stunning navy blue dress that brought out her eyes. Everyone was quiet, which was groundbreaking in and of itself.

With three kids, this almost never happened.

I thought about everything I'd been learning in therapy, and I had this realization: *You're doing it.*

There I was at church, a 38-year-old dad, the

same age as my parents when my father started to become addicted to painkillers and their marriage started to take the first steps toward falling apart.

But that wasn't my life. Mel and I had been together for sixteen years, and I loved and respected her, and I honestly admired her as a human, mother, and thinker. Our three kids were challenging, sure, but on the whole, they were good-natured goofballs who I genuinely enjoyed having around, and I was invested in their development.

I was raising a family in a calm and stable home, something I longed for as a child but never had. It was a warm feeling of satisfaction that I didn't exactly go looking for but somehow found in that moment.

I don't often allow myself to feel pride, honestly. I think having a challenging childhood combined with a life with mental illness can make emotions like pride difficult to acknowledge. I'm often afraid to feel too confident, too secure, too proud, too happy, because I know that things can get bad at any moment. I've seen it happen, so I try to keep those emotions in check, almost like I'm keeping my guard up, because then the distance between the positive emotions and the eventual letdown won't be such a huge gap. And now that I've written all of that down, I don't know if it makes any sense to anyone but me. But what I know for sure is this: That is a terrible way to look at life, and I should just allow myself to be happy, and proud, and positive and let those emotions be free from the possibility of future negative emotions.

But hey . . . I'm still working on that.

I'm still working on a lot, actually.

But in that moment, I allowed myself to feel pretty proud not only of my family but also of myself.

I thought about all the times I prayed for God to remove my anxiety disorder. But in this moment, I had a realization. Asking God to reach into my head and fix my mental illness is what I really, honestly, truly want him to do, but it's not how God does things. At least not in my experience. My anxiety is my burden to bear. It will be with me until I die. I've accepted that. But what God can do is help me lift the load, and through using the skills I'd acquired in therapy, along with finding the right medications, I'd found the sanity to have this absolutely wonderful family sitting next to me. And all of that felt like a huge blessing.

And as I thought about all of this, I recalled the conversation I'd had with my old Pizza Hut manager years ago. I was so envious of his family, and I realized that I was now doing something I never thought was possible. I was raising a family in a stable and happy home. And I know, there are some of you reading this and feeling like it's about to turn into a spiritual book. But this is the end of my story, so don't get too overwhelmed with my sudden testimony.

Sure, I still had anxiety, I knew that. But I also felt confidence in knowing that I had the tools to manage it, both religious and practical, and that realization helped me feel confident in knowing that I'd always be there for my wife and children.

In this moment, I knew that the greatest gift I could offer my family was learning to manage my mental illness in a healthy and responsible way, so that I could have enough of myself available to be a nurturing father and husband.

Near the end of the church service, I put my arm around my youngest, and she leaned into my side. She put her arms around me and gave me the tightest squeeze.

I leaned down and whispered, "I love you, kiddo."

She didn't respond.

She just squeezed me tighter.

ACKNOWLEDGMENTS

The first essay I ever wrote was in English 1010, a class I was very nervous to take because I'd always assumed I was bad at writing. The first assignment was to write a personal essay, so I chose to write about the time I pooped my pants in freshman PE. Surprisingly, the essay received an A, along with a note from the instructor telling me how awesome it was. That was almost sixteen years ago. What I didn't realize at the time, however, is that I'd started writing this book. Sixteen years is a long time to work on a project, and over the years, this sucker has passed through a lot of hands and I have a lot of people to thank. Hopefully I've captured them all.

Steven Fullmer, Karin Anderson, Lee Mortensen, Scott Hatch, Kate McPherson, thank you for your kind edits and support early in this project.

Amber Smith-Johnson, Brandon Henderson, Jimmy Neel, Liz Watson Christianson, and Loz Cook, you were my first writing friends and a true inspiration.

Geoff Herbach, Candice Black, Diana Joseph, Richard Terrill, Roger Sheffer, and Richard Robbins, thank you for your inspiration during graduate school.

Sarah Johnson, Kara Garbe Balcerzak, Caitlin O'Sullivan, Melody Heide, Angie Johnson, and Matt Oliver, my MFA buddies, thank you for three full years of thoughtful critiques.

JT Bushnell, thank you for reading and editing that early draft.

Geoff Berg, Caleb West, Elijah Brown, Helen Naegle, Bryce Arnold, Vern Tanner and Brad Tanner, and Claire Nicogossian, thank you for lending your expertise.

Thank you to the Greens for always being interested and giving the jokes in my writing more laughter than they probably deserve.

Justin Day, thank you for allowing me to complain about this book endlessly on our never-ending bike rides.

Thank you to Jan and Steve at Folio for helping me finally solidify this concept and title.

To the nearly 200 agents and editors who rejected this project over the years, as much as I hate to say it, I do owe you something, because your rejection pushed me to keep looking at this book from different angles.

Marissa, my editor, thank you for your continued support. You keep believing in me for reasons I cannot explain but deeply appreciate. I believe that same sentiment can be directed at all the good people at Page Street Publishing.

Thank you to Mel for being all-around amazing and supportive and hands down the most wonderful person in my life.

ABOUT THE AUTHOR

Clint Edwards is the celebrated author of *Father-ish*, *Silence is a Scary Sound*, and *I'm Sorry...Love, Your Husband*. He writes the weekly column *Screen Time* hosted by Netflix and is the founder of the wildly popular daddy blog *No Idea What I'm Doing*. He was the 2021 Iris Awards dad blogger of the year, and his stories have been featured in the *New York Times*, *The Washington Post*, *People*, *Redbook*, *Good Morning America*, and *The Today Show*. He lives in Lebanon, Oregon, with his wife and three children.